ANDERSON'S
Law School Publications

Administrative Law Anthology
Thomas O. Sargentich

Administrative Law: Cases and Materials
Daniel J. Gifford

Alternative Dispute Resolution: Strategies for Law and Business
E. Wendy Trachte-Huber and Stephen K. Huber

American Legal Systems: A Resource and Reference Guide
Toni M. Fine

An Admiralty Law Anthology
Robert M. Jarvis

Analytic Jurisprudence Anthology
Anthony D'Amato

An Antitrust Anthology
Andrew I. Gavil

Appellate Advocacy: Principles and Practice: Cases and Materials, Second Edition
Ursula Bentele and Eve Cary

Basic Accounting Principles for Lawyers: With Present Value and Expected Value
C. Steven Bradford and Gary A. Ames

A Capital Punishment Anthology (and Electronic Caselaw Appendix)
Victor L. Streib

Cases and Problems in Criminal Law, Third Edition
Myron Moskovitz

The Citation Workbook: How to Beat the Citation Blues, Second Edition
Maria L. Ciampi, Rivka Widerman, and Vicki Lutz

Civil Procedure: Cases, Materials, and Questions
Richard D. Freer and Wendy C. Perdue

Clinical Anthology: Readings for Live-Client Clinics
Alex J. Hurder, Frank S. Bloch, Susan L. Brooks, and Susan L. Kay

Commercial Transactions: Problems and Materials
Louis F. Del Duca, Egon Guttman, Alphonse M. Squillante, Fred H. Miller, and Peter Winship
    Vol. 1: Secured Transactions Under the UCC
    Vol. 2: Sales Under the UCC and the CISG
    Vol. 3: Negotiable Instruments Under the UCC and the CIBN

Communications Law: Media, Entertainment, and Regulation
Donald E. Lively, Allen S. Hammond, IV, Blake D. Morant, and Russell L. Weaver

A Conflict-of-Laws Anthology
Gene R. Shreve

A Constitutional Law Anthology, Second Edition
Donald E. Lively, Michael J. Glennon, Phoebe A. Haddon, Dorothy E. Roberts, and Russell L. Weaver

Constitutional Conflicts, Parts I & II
Derrick A. Bell, Jr.

Constitutional Law: Cases, History, and Dialogues
Donald E. Lively, Phoebe A. Haddon, Dorothy E. Roberts, and Russell L. Weaver

The Constitutional Law of the European Union
James D. Dinnage and John F. Murphy

The Constitutional Law of the European Union: Documentary Supplement
James D. Dinnage and John F. Murphy

Constitutional Torts
Sheldon H. Nahmod, Michael L. Wells, and Thomas A. Eaton

Contracts
Contemporary Cases, Comments, and Problems
Michael L. Closen, Richard M. Perlmutter, and Jeffrey D. Wittenberg

A Contracts Anthology, Second Edition
Peter Linzer

A Corporate Law Anthology
Franklin A. Gevurtz

Corporate and White Collar Crime: An Anthology
Leonard Orland

A Criminal Law Anthology
Arnold H. Loewy

Criminal Law: Cases and Materials
Arnold H. Loewy

A Criminal Procedure Anthology
Silas J. Wasserstrom and Christie L. Snyder

Criminal Procedure: Arrest and Investigation
Arnold H. Loewy and Arthur B. LaFrance

Criminal Procedure: Trial and Sentencing
Arthur B. LaFrance and Arnold H. Loewy

Economic Regulation: Cases and Materials
Richard J. Pierce, Jr.

Elements of Law
Eva H. Hanks, Michael E. Herz, and Steven S. Nemerson

Ending It: Dispute Resolution in America
Descriptions, Examples, Cases and Questions
Susan M. Leeson and Bryan M. Johnston

Environmental Law, Second Edition
Jackson B. Battle, Robert L. Fischman, Maxine I. Lipeles, and Mark S. Squillace
    Vol. 1: Environmental Decisionmaking: NEPA and the Endangered Species Act
    Vol. 2: Water Pollution
    Vol. 3: Air Pollution
    Vol. 4: Hazardous Waste

An Environmental Law Anthology
Robert L. Fischman, Maxine I. Lipeles, and Mark S. Squillace

Environmental Protection and Justice
Readings and Commentary on Environmental Law and Practice
Kenneth A. Manaster

An Evidence Anthology
Edward J. Imwinkelried and Glen Weissenberger

Federal Evidence Courtroom Manual
Glen Weissenberger

Federal Income Tax Anthology
Paul L. Caron, Karen C. Burke, and Grayson M.P. McCouch

Federal Rules of Evidence, 1996-97 Edition
Rules, Legislative History, Commentary and Authority
Glen Weissenberger

Federal Rules of Evidence Handbook, 1996-97 Edition
Publisher's Staff

First Amendment Anthology
Donald E. Lively, Dorothy E. Roberts, and Russell L. Weaver

International Environmental Law Anthology
Anthony D'Amato and Kirsten Engel

International Human Rights: Law, Policy and Process, Second Edition
Frank C. Newman and David Weissbrodt

**Selected International Human Rights Instruments and
Bibliography For Research on International Human Rights Law, Second Edition**
Frank C. Newman and David Weissbrodt

International Intellectual Property Anthology
Anthony D'Amato and Doris Estelle Long

International Law Anthology
Anthony D'Amato

International Law Coursebook
Anthony D'Amato

Introduction to The Study of Law: Cases and Materials
John Makdisi

Judicial Externships: The Clinic Inside The Courthouse
Rebecca A. Cochran

Justice and the Legal System
A Coursebook
Anthony D'Amato and Arthur J. Jacobson

The Law of Disability Discrimination
Ruth Colker

ADA Handbook
Statutes, Regulations and Related Materials
Publisher's Staff

The Law of Modern Payment Systems and Notes
Fred H. Miller and Alvin C. Harrell

Lawyers and Fundamental Moral Responsibility
Daniel R. Coquillette

Microeconomic Predicates to Law and Economics
Mark Seidenfeld

Patients, Psychiatrists and Lawyers Law and the Mental Health System, Second Edition
Raymond L. Spring, Roy B. Lacoursiere, M.D., and Glen Weissenberger

Preventive Law: Materials on a Non Adversarial Legal Process
Robert M. Hardaway

Principles of Evidence, Third Edition
Irving Younger, Michael Goldsmith, and David A. Sonenshein

Problems and Simulations in Evidence, Second Edition
Thomas F. Guernsey

A Products Liability Anthology
Anita Bernstein

Professional Responsibility Anthology
Thomas B. Metzloff

A Property Anthology, Second Edition
Richard H. Chused

Public Choice and Public Law: Readings and Commentary
Maxwell L. Stearns

The Regulation of Banking
Cases and Materials on Depository Institutions and Their Regulators
Michael P. Malloy

Science in Evidence
David H. Kaye

A Section 1983 Civil Rights Anthology
Sheldon H. Nahmod

Sports Law: Cases and Materials, Third Edition
Ray L. Yasser, James R. McCurdy, and C. Peter Goplerud

A Torts Anthology
Lawrence C. Levine, Julie A. Davies, and Edward J. Kionka

Trial Practice
Lawrence A. Dubin and Thomas F. Guernsey

Trial Practice Problems and Case Files
Edward R. Stein and Lawrence A. Dubin

Trial Practice and Case Files *with Video* Presentation
Edward R. Stein and Lawrence A. Dubin

Unincorporated Business Entities
Larry E. Ribstein

FORTHCOMING PUBLICATIONS

Antitrust Law: Cases and Materials
Daniel J. Gifford and Leo J. Raskind

A Civil Procedure Anthology
David I. Levine, Donald L. Doernberg, and Melissa L. Nelken

Civil Procedure: Cases, Materials, and Questions, 2nd Edition
Richard D. Freer and Wendy C. Perdue

Constitutional Law Anthology, 2nd Edition
Michael J Glenon, Donald E. Lively, Phoebe A. Haddon, Dorothy E. Roberts and Russell L. Weaver

Contract Law and Practice: Cases and Materials
Michael L. Closen, Gerald E. Berendt, Doris Estelle Long, Marie A. Monahan, Robert J. Nye, and John H. Scheid

European Union Law Anthology
Anthony D'Amato and Karen V. Kole

Family Law Anthology
Frances E. Olsen

Law and Economics: An Anthology
Kenneth G. Dau-Schmidt and Thomas S. Ulen

THE CITATION WORKBOOK
HOW TO BEAT THE CITATION BLUES
SECOND EDITION

THE CITATION WORKBOOK
HOW TO BEAT THE CITATION BLUES

SECOND EDITION

MARIA L. CIAMPI

RIVKA WIDERMAN

VICKI LUTZ

ANDERSON PUBLISHING CO.
CINCINNATI, OHIO

THE CITATION WORKBOOK: HOW TO BEAT THE CITATION BLUES, Second Edition
Maria L. Ciampi, Rivka Widerman, Vicki Lutz

© 1997 by Anderson Publishing Co.

Anderson Publishing Co.
2035 Reading Road / Cincinnati, Ohio 45202
800-582-7295 / e-mail andpubco@aol.com / Fax 513-562-5430

ISBN: 0-87084-139-4

Table of Contents

Preface

Learning proper citation form is an integral part of any legal writing program. Proper citation form, however, is difficult to teach and frustrating to learn. This book is written for and dedicated to those law professors who teach, and to those students who must master, legal citations. Do not give up hope yet—help is on the way!

Introduction

In 1993, we published *The Citation Workbook: How to Beat the Citation Blues,* a tool for guiding professors and teachers through the arcane world of legal citations. Now we bring you a second edition of *How to Beat the Citation Blues.* The first edition drew an immediately gratifying response. So why did we choose to revise a good thing?

Most obviously, the release of the sixteenth edition of the *Uniform System of Citation* ("the Bluebook") necessitated some changes, but even without the appearance of a new edition of the Bluebook, we would be tempted to revise *How to Beat the Citation Blues.*

When we first wrote *How to Beat the Citation Blues* four years ago, teaching citations seemed simple: get your students to master the Bluebook along with an understanding of the nature of basic legal sources. Since then legal research and, so, citations have become more complicated. Legal research is no longer confined to books and periodicals or even to the granddaddies of electronic databases, LEXIS and WESTLAW. Legal documents are now found on the Internet and on CD-ROMs. As a matter of fact, law is all over cyberspace. Law libraries, *e.g.*, <http://www.veruslaw.com>, and government depository sites, *e.g.*, <http://thorpus.lib.purdue.edu/gpo>, have sprung up in cyberspace. Sources, such as municipal codes, that once might have required a trip to city hall are now readily available. *E.g.*, <http://pen.ci.santa-monica.ca./us>. Some of these Internet sources are for subscribers only, but many are free.

We do not recommend using the Internet or the WWW as a primary source of legal research. The data available is usually limited in scope, scattered over a large number of sites and often transitory. It does not make for efficient research.[1] The Bluebook also does not recommend relying on the Internet, but its editors have come to realize, as we have, that increasingly computer savvy generations of lawyers, law students and paralegals are going to use the Internet to access information. And so the sixteenth edition of the Bluebook has created a new rule, **Rule 17.3.3**, for citations to authority found on the Internet.

The surge in electronic sources has prompted another change in the Bluebook, the recognition of the primacy of universal citations, referred to in the Bluebook as medium neutral or official public domain citations when available. **Rule 10.3.1.** Unfortunately the Bluebook does not clearly explain what a medium neutral or public domain citation is, although it

---

[1] A guidebook to law on the Internet does exist, appropriately titled LAW ON THE NET by James Evans and published by Nolo Press. The caveats stated above still apply since information about sites on the Internet can be obsolete almost as soon as it is published.

does give a couple of examples of what it might look like. We try to fill that gap in this revised edition. *See* Part III of *How to Beat the Citation Blues*.

The sixteenth edition of the Bluebook contains a number of other changes. Most of these will not significantly affect beginning legal research and writing curricula, with one exception: **Rule 1.2** (regarding the use of signals). The editors of the sixteenth edition have revised **Rule 1.2** to eliminate the signal *contra* and to modify the definitions of no signal and the signal *see*. These changes have engendered a great deal of controversy among teachers and writers of the law. We come down on the side of those who oppose these changes; we believe that they encourage muddy analysis. We have, therefore, retained the rules for signals from the fifteenth edition of the Bluebook and have added definitions and examples in Part VI, "Putting It All Together."

The basic format of *How to Beat the Citation Blues* has not changed. It is still essentially a workbook designed to teach students proper legal citation form for the basic types of legal writing learned during the first year of law school and in paralegal programs: the client letter, the interoffice memorandum and the appellate brief. It is still designed to be a "workbook" with the exercises to be done in the book itself, but it is now divided into six parts instead of four. Part I of the workbook is entitled "Getting Started" and provides an overview of the Bluebook. Part I consists of two exercises, which introduce students to the basic kinds of legal material and basic citation form for each such material. In Part II, "Citation Placement and Frequency," students learn to use citation sentences and clauses in the written text, beginning to mirror what they will have to do in real writing assignments. Part III describes public domain or universal citations. Part IV, "Welcome to Cyberspace," contains an exercise in citing to sources found on the Internet and on electronic databases. Part V contains a series of exercises that teach students "short form" citations. In Part VI, "Putting It All Together," students must use all the rules mastered in two final exercises, as well as the definitions of signals that we prefer. Part VI also introduces students to some of the nuances of legal citation. The workbook's appendix now contains a sample trial memorandum of law.

In short, *How to Beat the Citation Blues* will continue to give students the basics they need to know and the security that they have mastered them.

PART I
GETTING STARTED

The first year of law school can be very puzzling, and even frightening, to many law students. *The Bluebook*: *A Uniform System of Citation* (the "Bluebook"), unfortunately, sometimes adds to the emotional turbulence that students experience. Part of the reason for this is that students do not know how to start tackling the fairly complex system of legal citation contained in the Bluebook—indeed, frequently they are not even familiar with the types of materials they are being asked to cite.

You will not really become familiar with the various types of legal materials until you actually use them. Part I will attempt, however, to summarize for you the basic types of legal materials and to introduce you to the basic rules of citation for these various materials.

Basic Citation Form

Introduction

The Bluebook provides you with the rules governing the correct form of legal citation for virtually every type of legal, and even a good deal of non-legal, authority. The Bluebook is divided into rules which are organized under the headings indicated on the back outside cover. The front inside cover of the Bluebook is a quick reference for law review footnote citations, while the back inside cover is a quick reference for court documents and legal memoranda.

During this year you will probably use the rules and typefaces for court documents and legal memoranda, not those for law review footnotes. One feature of the Bluebook that will help you on this score is Chapter P (light blue pages) for practitioners, which summarizes the Bluebook rules to be used for these documents.[1] Another important feature of the Bluebook for the student, law review editor and practitioner alike is that it is cross-referenced for rules and Tables (part T).

Take a look at the "Introduction to Legal Citation and the Bluebook." **I.1** and **I.2** set forth the Bluebook's structure as well as general principles of citation. The rest of this part discusses the use of citations in a general way and sets forth the basic citation format for the major types of legal authority (cases, constitutions, statutes, rules, regulations, books, periodicals).

The first two citation exercises, the "French Revolution" Exercise and Citation Exercise #2, introduce you to the major types of legal authorities and the legal citation form for each of these authorities. Notice that each citation is in "sentence" form, ending with a period. In the "French Revolution" Exercise, also note that each "sentence" begins with a "signal," something you have probably never seen before. The signal identifies the relationship between the authority you are citing and the text. Although the "French Revolution" Exercise does not contain any text, it does include signals to get you used to seeing them and to force you to read about them in **I.3** and **Rules 1.3[2] to 1.4** of the Bluebook.

---

[1] Be careful, therefore, to apply these rules, and not those for law review footnotes, in doing your assignments. Note well that the examples given in the Bluebook under specific rules sometimes follow the typeface conventions for law reviews rather than those for court documents and legal memoranda; always refer to Chapter P and the inside back cover for proper practitioner typeface conventions.

[2] We disagree with the definition of signals stated in Rule 1.2 of the sixteenth edition of the Bluebook, *see* Introduction, xiv, and urge you to use the definitions stated in Part VI, "Putting It All Together," of this book.

"French Revolution" Citation Exercise #1

Each of the citations below contains one or more errors. Please correct each citation according to the sixteenth edition of *The Bluebook: A Uniform System of Citation* (the "Bluebook"). Write the corrected citation on line a. and the governing rule(s) for each correction on line b. Use the citation rules applicable to court documents and legal memoranda, not those for law review footnotes.

1. Louis v. Marie Antoinette, 10 F.Supp. 932 (S.D.N.Y. C.D. 1978).

   a. _____

   _____

   b. _____

   _____

2. E.g. Mirabeau v. Turgot, Beaumarchais v. Robespierre, 12 F. 2d 135 (C.C.A.9th 1981).
   9th Cir   10.4

   a. _____

   _____

   b. _____

   _____

3. Accord Estate of M. de Launey, 38 A.2d 222 (1971), affirmed, 48 A.2d 151 (1971).

   a. _____

   _____

   b. _____

   _____

4. See In the Matter of M. Lafayette, 59 S.W. 2d 766.

   a. _____

   _____

   b. _____

   _____

5. See also, Talleyrand v. De Launey et al., 109 U.S. 324 (1978).

a. _____

_____

b. _____

_____

compare

6. Cf., J. Necker v. The King, Trustee, 103 So.2d 500, 501 (1965) (Chief Justice Robespierre dissenting).

a. _____

_____

b. _____

_____

7. But see *The Peasant's act*, 18 U. S. C. §120(m) (1968).

a. _____

_____

b. _____

_____

8. But see Ciampi, Maria L., Where King Louis Went Wrong: How the Monarchy Could Have Won the French Revolution, 63 *L'Etat L.Rev.* 71, 75-6 (1990).

a. _____

_____

b. _____

_____

9. But cf., J. Rousseau, The Death of Marie Antoinette p. 25 note 6 (1989).

a. _____

_____

b. _____

_____

10. See generally 5 F. Voltaire & C. Montesquieu, The Makings of A
Revolution paragraphs 190-95 (1979).

a. _____

_____

b. _____

_____

11. See, e.g., Maximilien Robespierre, Jacobin Election Council, visited July 14, 2089, http://frenchrevolution.gov/robespierre

a. _____

_____

b. _____

_____

Citation Exercise #2

Each of the citations below contains one or more errors. Please correct each citation according to the sixteenth edition of *The Bluebook: A Uniform System of Citation* (the "Bluebook"). Write the corrected citation on line a. and the governing rule(s) for each correction on line b. Use the citation rules applicable to court documents and legal memoranda, not those for law review footnotes.

1. Article 2, Section 3, clause 1 of the United States Constitution.

   a. _____

   _____

   b. _____

   _____

2. Fifth amendment to the United States Constitution.

   a. _____

   _____

   b. _____

   _____

3. Preamble of the Oklahoma constitution.

   a. _____

   _____

   b. _____

   _____

4. Sections 848 and 853 of title 21 of the United States Code, published in 1988.

   a. _____

   _____

   b. _____

   _____

5. Chapter 119, Section 51A of the Annotated Laws of Massachu-
    setts, published in 1975 with a supplement in 1986.

    a. _____

    _____

    b. _____

    _____

6. Uniform Commercial Code, Section 4-101, published in 1985.

    a. _____

    _____

    b. _____

    _____

7. Disciplinary rule 5-106(c) of the Model Code of Professional
    Responsibility, published in 1980.

    a. _____

    _____

    b. _____

    _____

8. Senate Report number 225, by the 98th Congress, First Session
    at 8 in 1984, reprinted in 1984, United States Code Congres-
    sional and Administrative News 3372 at p. 3374.

    a. _____

    _____

    b. _____

    _____

9. E. Allan Farnsworth, Contracts, Section 2396, published by
    McNaughton as revised in 1961.

    a. _____

    _____

    b. _____

    _____

10. Communications to Clergymen—When Are They Privileged, by Michael Kuhlmann, a 1968 Valparaiso University Law Review, volume 2, p. 265.

a. _____

_____

b. _____

_____

11. Bingo Games, sec.6.100.030 Santa Monica, Ca. Municipal Code (last modified Sept. 10, 1996), http://pen.ci.santa-monica..ca.us/city/municode/art06/6.100/index.html

a. _____

_____

b. _____

_____

PART II
CITATION PLACEMENT AND FREQUENCY

Now that you have mastered the basic forms of citation, you are probably wondering how to use them. The next two exercises are designed to teach you where and how often to use citations in a legal document.

In legal writing, citations appear with great frequency. Every time you quote or paraphrase an authority, legal or otherwise, secondary or primary, you must cite to that authority. Virtually every statement you make about the law which you have derived from a source other than your own imagination requires a citation. For example, if you write, "Courts require that a collection agency give notice to a debtor before it repossesses his car," you must follow that statement with a citation to the courts' opinions which have required such notice. The statement and citation would look like this:

> Courts require that a collection agency give notice to a debtor before it repossesses his car. *Turner v. Colonial Fin. Corp.,* 467 F.2d 202, 203 (7th Cir. 1972); *Inter City Motor Sales v. Szymanski,* 42 Mich. App. 112, 114, 201 N.W.2d 378, 381 (1972).

Another alternative would be to write it like this:

> Courts require that a collection agency give notice to a debtor before it repossesses his car. *E.g., Very Used Car Loans v. Doe*, 1 F.3d 100 (14th Cir. 2001).

A citation that follows a complete sentence, as do the previous examples, is known as a citation sentence. It immediately follows the period at the end of the sentence to which it cites or refers and is in turn followed by a period.

You may also want to list several authorities in a **citation sentence**, as in the first example above. **Rules 1.3 and 1.4** of the Bluebook explain the order in which authorities must appear.

Sometimes a citation sentence will begin with a signal, a word or abbreviation such as "E.g.," as in the second example above, or "See." Signals tell the reader how much weight he or she should give to the authority referred to in the citation sentence. For an introduction to signals, refer to Part VI, "Putting It All Together."

A citation can also appear within a sentence and is then known as a **citation clause** or as a **citation within a sentence**. For example, if you write the sentence, "In the case of *Palsgraf v. Long Island R.R. Co.,* 248 N.Y. 339, 162 N.E. 99 (1922), Justice Cardozo gave the classical definition of proximate cause," you are writing a citation within a sentence. The citation plays a grammatical role within the sentence; it functions as the object of the preposition "in."

The next two exercises will give you the opportunity to implement these basic rules of citation placement. Each exercise contains a paragraph with no citations followed by a list of authorities. You will use each authority to create a citation in the appropriate spot in the paragraph. Here is an example before you begin.

Sample citation placement exercise:

In 1905, the state of Indiana prohibited the sale, manufacture, and possession of cigarettes. The statute, however, specifically exempted cigarettes which only passed through the state. The United States Supreme Court had held several years earlier that states could not use their anti-cigarette laws to interfere with interstate commerce. Not long after passage of the statute, the Indiana state supreme court held that the statute also did not apply to individual adults who had obtained cigarettes outside the state but possessed them within the state. The Indiana legislature repealed the cigarette prohibition in 1909.

Authorities:

Repeal of Anti-Cigarette Law, ch. 28, 1909 Ind. Acts 266.

Austin v. Tennessee, 170 U.S. 343 (1900).

Ind. Code Ann. § 2216 (Michie 1905).

Id.

State v. Lowry, 166 Ind. 372, 77 N.E. 728 (1906).

Sample Answer:

In 1905, the state of Indiana prohibited the sale, manufacture, and possession of cigarettes. Ind. Code Ann. § 2216 (Michie 1905). The statute, however, specifically exempted cigarettes which only passed through the state. *Id.* The United States Supreme Court had held several years earlier that states could not use their anti-cigarette laws to interfere with interstate commerce. *Austin v. Tennessee,* 170 U.S. 343 (1900). Not long after passage of the statute, the Indiana state supreme court held that the statute also did not apply to individual adults who had obtained cigarettes outside the state but possessed them within the state. *State v. Lowry,* 166 Ind. 372, 77 N.E. 728 (1906). The Indiana legislature repealed the cigarette prohibition in 1909. Repeal of Anti-Cigarette Law, ch. 28, 1909 Ind. Acts 266.

Explanation:

Ind. Code Ann. § 2216 (Michie 1905).: The first citation to the Indiana code supplies the authority for the statement about the state's prohibition of cigarettes. It tells you where you can find the provisions of the state's prohibition.

Id.: The second citation provides the source of the exception to the prohibition which is to the statute already cited. "*Id.*" means that the citation is the same as the previous one.

Austin v. Tennessee, 170 U.S. 343 (1900).: The third citation sentence is to the United States Supreme Court case which predated the Indiana statute and would therefore have to limit the statute's scope.

State v. Lowry, 166 Ind. 372, 77 N.E. 728 (1906).: The fourth citation is to an Indiana state supreme court case which, in interpreting the statute, added another exception to the prohibition.

Repeal of Anti-Cigarette Law, ch. 28, 1909 Ind. Acts 266.: The fifth citation sentence is to the state statutes at large or session laws, the designation given to statutes in the legislature before they are formally codified by subject and renumbered in the state's code. Session laws which repeal statutes are rarely codified; however, you can often find a citation to them in the place in the code where the repealed statutes originally appeared.

In the following two exercises, please indicate where you place a citation and the authority you would use by using an insertion sign ∧ and placing the appropriate citation above it. The double-spacing of the paragraph in each exercise will allow you to do this. Be sure to use citation sentences where appropriate and citation clauses where appropriate, making any necessary changes in the text and in the citation.

Citation Exercise #3

In 1990, Congress passed legislation requiring nutrition labeling on all non-meat food products sold in the United States. Pursuant to this act, the Food and Drug Administration proposed regulations that would standardize the definitions of terms commonly used in the labeling of packaged foods, such as "low in fat." The regulations also proposed standardizing the serving sizes of common foods as they appeared on the label. Although the legislation did not cover meat and meat products that are under the jurisdiction of the United States Department of Agriculture, that agency announced that it would change the labeling requirements for meat products to avoid consumer confusion. The Food and Drug Administration's nutrition labeling regulations were not finalized until early 1993.

Authorities:

1. Food Labeling: Nutrient Content Claims, General Principles, Petitions, Definitions of Terms, 56 Fed. Reg. 60,421 (1991) (to be codified at 21 C.F.R. pt. 101) (proposed Nov. 27, 1991).

2. Food Labeling: Serving Sizes, 56 Fed. Reg. 60,394 (1991) (to be codified at 21 C.F.R. §§ 101.8, 101.9) (proposed Nov. 27, 1991).

3. Food Labeling Regulations Implementing the Nutrition Labeling and Education Act of 1990, 58 Fed. Reg. 2066 (1993) (to be codified at 21 C.F.R. pts. 5, 20, 100, 101, 105, 130).

4. Nutrition Labeling and Education Act, Pub. L. No. 101-535, § l(a), 194 Stat. 2353 (1990) (codified at 21 U.S.C. § 343 (1996)).

5. Nutrition Labeling of Meat and Poultry Products, 56 Fed. Reg. 60,302 (1991) (to be codified at 9 C.F.R. §§ 317.1-317.5) (proposed Nov. 27, 1991).

Citation Exercise #4

The Constitution provides for three distinct branches of government. The doctrine that motivated this form of governmental organization is known as separation of powers, and its purpose, to quote Justice Brandeis, is "not to promote efficiency but to preclude the exercise of arbitrary power." Although legal commentators have written about the effect of the doctrine of separation of powers on the law, the courts continue to grapple with the constitutional questions this doctrine raises as the legislative and executive branches have grown and become more complex.

Authorities :

1. *see, e.g., INS v. Chadha*, 462 U.S. 919 (1983) (declaring legislative veto of INS administrative action unconstitutional because it violated separation of powers between legislative and executive branches).

2. *Myers v. United States*, 272 U.S. 52, 293 (1926) (Brandeis, J., dissenting).

3. *see, e.g.*, Paul R. Verkuil, *Separation of Powers, The Rule of Law and the Idea of Independence*, 30 Wm. & Mary L. Rev. 301 (1989).

4. U.S. Const. arts. I-III.

PART III
THE OFFICIAL PUBLIC DOMAIN OR UNIVERSAL CITATION

According to **Rule 10.3.1** of the Bluebook, an official "public domain" or "medium neutral" citation is a citation that will enable a researcher to find an authority in any form in which it might appear, be it in a bound volume or on an electronic database. Such citations are also called "vendor neutral" or "universal" citations. We will use the term universal citation because that is the term adopted by the American Bar Association and the Association of American Law Libraries ("AALL").

The growing reliance by lawyers, legal scholars and paralegals on electronically available data has caused many to rethink the form that citations should take. Especially for cases, treatises and journals, citations assume that the authority will be found in a bound volume with specified number of pages and published in a particular year. Electronic media like online databases or CD-ROMs can make legal authority more widely and less expensively available. The AALL has, therefore, encouraged the development and use of universal citations.[1] The universal citation described in **Rule 10.3.1** is based on the AALL's proposed form.

South Dakota and Maine have adopted a universal citation in the form modeled on the AALL proposal; they differ somewhat in the use of spacing and paragraph symbols. Both states also require a parallel cite, but only to the first page; pinpoint or jump cites are to the paragraph number even when a parallel cite refers to a bound reporter. If you are writing for a Maine or South Dakota court, you should check the court rules for the proper citation form. Louisiana also has adopted a universal citation system, but *it differs from that proposed by the AALL as well as the form implied by Table I of the Bluebook*. If you are writing for a Louisiana court, you should check the court rules for proper citation form.

A few states are actively opposed to the introduction of a universal citation, while others, such as Wisconsin (the format used by the AALL is the one developed by proponents of a universal citation in Wisconsin), Florida, Tennessee, Arizona and Arkansas are considering proposals to adopt a universal citation as their official citation.

So far, universal citations have only been devised for court opinions; more are being developed for other types of authority. The AALL also has two subcommittees of its Committee on Citation Format working on universal citations for statutes and regulations. Because the form described in the Bluebook may be somewhat sketchy, we have provided

---

[1] Because the format as proposed by the AALL would not be copyrightable, the AALL had referred to medium neutral citations as vendor neutral citations, and the Bluebook provides the alternative term of public domain citation.

rules for universal citations of court opinions as devised by the AALL. American Association of Law Libraries, *User Guide to the AALL Medium Neutral Citation, Case Citations February, 1996* (visited Dec. 16, 1996) <http://www.aallnet.org>.[2]

At present, universal citation forms exist only for cases.

Rule 1. Basic Citation Form. [Supplementary to Blue Book **Rule 10.1**.]

Rules in parentheses refer to rules of the AALL universal citation system, not the Bluebook.

A full case citation includes:

1. the case name (**Rule 2**)
2. the year of decision (**Rule 3**)
3. the court (**Rule 4**)
4. the opinion number (**Rule 5**)
5. the notation U—if the opinion is unreported (**Rule 6**)
6. the paragraph number—if a pinpoint cite is needed to specific text (**Rule 7**)

Examples:

Godard v. Poole, 1995 US 353, 23
Price v. Bitner, 1996 Wis 404, 12
Cohen v. Estes, 1998 US Mich (W Dist) 90, 44
Billings v. Kehoe, 1999 La Ascension Parish 104U, 12
Roalfe v. Houdek, 2000 NY Sur (11th) 112, 245

Rule 2. Case Name. [Supplementary to Bluebook **Rule 10.2**.]

Case names should conform to **Rule 10.2** and related rules of the Bluebook—except that a researcher may cite an opinion from any source so long as it contains the data elements used in the AALL universal citation.

Rule 3. Year of Decision. [Supplementary to Bluebook **Rule 10.5**.]

After the case name, indicate the year in which the decision was rendered. Express the year as a four digit number, *e.g.*, 1995 not 95.

Rule 4. Court. [Supplementary to the Bluebook **Rule 10.4**.]

After the year, indicate the court which rendered the opinion. Identify the court with an abbreviation using the sub-rules below.

---

[2] Reprinted with permission.

1. Generally, use **US** to identify a federal court. Use the standard geographical abbreviations from the latest edition of the Bluebook to identify a state or territorial court.

2. Also use standardized abbrevations from the Bluebook when needed to identify local or specialized courts.

3. Omit periods and other punctuation within the court abbreviation as they are superfluous. *E.g.*, use US not U.S.

Omit the abbreviation Ct—unless its omission would make the abbreviation ambiguous.

Rule 4.1 High Courts.

Identify a high court decision by using only a geographical abbrevation.

For example, use **US** to cite a United States Supreme Court decision and Miss—not Ms—to cite a Mississsippi Supreme Court decision.

Examples:

1699 **US** 212, 8

1997 **Miss** 33, 17

Rule 4.2 Intermediate Appellate Courts of General Jurisdiction.

To cite an appellate court:

1. use **US** or a state or territorial abbreviation,

2. followed by App.,

3. followed by the number or name of the judicial circuit or district in parentheses, *e.g.*, US App (**11th**) or US App (**DC**). Omit the parenthetical if the circuit or district is part of a unitary appellate court and its opinion binds all coequal divisions of the court.

Omit the abbreviations Cir or Dist unless the omission would make the abbreviation ambiguous.

Examples:

1997 **US App (8th)** 33, 17

1996 **La App (5th)** 212, 8

Rule 4.3 Other Courts.

To cite any trial court or a specialized appellate court:

1a. use **US** for a federal court—followed by a state or territorial abbreviation if needed to identify a federal district,

Example: 1995 **US Mich (W Dist)** 111, 10

or   1b.   use a state or territorial abbreviation—followed by a local geographical abbreviation if needed to identify the local court issuing the opinion,

Example: 1999 **Miss Adams County** 33, 17

2.   followed by any additional standard abbreviations needed to unambiguously identify the court issuing the opinion,

Examples: 1996 **La Dist (10th)** 212, 8

1998 **Del Fam** 212, 8

3.   followed by the number or name of the judicial circuit or district in parentheses, *e.g.*, US App (11th) or US App (DC). Omit the parenthetical if the circuit or district is part of a unitary appellate court and its opinion binds all coequal divisions of the court.

Example: 2000 **NY Sur (11th)** 440, 5

Rule 5. Opinion Number. [No Equivalent Bluebook Rule.]

Courts supporting the AALL universal citation will apply a unique number to each opinion. Include this opinion number after the court abbreviation.

Example: 1996 US **212**, 8

Rule 6. Unreported Status. [Related to Bluebook **Rule 10.8.1**.]

If an opinion is unreported (as determined by the issuing jurisdiction), append the letter "U" to the opinion number.

Example: 1996 Ohio App (8th) 312U, 15

Rule 7. Pinpoint Citation by Paragraph Number (optional). [Related to Bluebook **Rule 3.3**.]

Courts supporting the AALL universal citation will number each paragraph of text within an opinion. After the opinion number, a researcher may cite to particular text by referring to the appropriate paragraph number. Place a comma between the opinion and paragraph numbers.

Example: 1996 US 212, **8**

PART IV
WELCOME TO CYBERSPACE

This part contains an exercise designed to teach you citation forms for authority found on the Internet and in electronic databases. As we stated in the introduction to this book, we do not recommend relying on the Internet for legal authority. Electronic databases such as LEXIS and WESTLAW are more comprehensive and reliable; however, the Internet can be useful for helping you track down background material.

The following exercise consists of several paragraphs from an interoffice memorandum. Each numbered citation contains at least one error. On the sheets that follow the exercise, correct the error(s) and state the Bluebook rule(s) you relied on.

"Hawaiian Sovereignty"
Citation Exercise # 5

In 1893, the Hawaiian monarchy was overthrown by rebel forces with the aid of the American government. Joan Beecher, Hawaii Sovereignty #1: The Apology Law, 5 Voice of America 62, Nov. 12, 1996, http://www.hawaii-nation.org/voa.html.[1] President Grover Cleveland denounced the overthrow as a "substantial wrong" that the United States "should endeavor to repair." Grover Cleveland, President of the United States, Message to U.S. Congress, http://hoohana.aloha.net/hsec/cleveland.html, visited October 13, 1996.[2]

Believing this substantial wrong was never repaired, many native Hawaiians sought to reassert sovereignty over the Hawaiian Islands. Their efforts first led to a joint resolution by Congress in 1993 formally acknowledging the centennial of the overthrow of the Kingdom of Hawaii and apologizing for the American government's role in it. Joint Resolution, November 23, 1993, Public Law Number 101-150, 107 Statutes at Large 1510, in LEXIS, through the 1996 legislation.[3] The joint resolution was called the "apology law." Joan Beecher, Hawaii Sovereignty #1: The Apology Law, 5 Voice of America 62, Nov. 12, 1996, http://www.hawaii-nation. org/voa.html; *see Rice v. Cayetano*, No. Civ. 96-00390 DAE, WESTLAW 1996, p. 88343, at *4, District Court of Hawaii, September 6, 1996.[4] Second, the state of Hawaii established the Hawaiian Sovereignty Elections

Council, whose mandate is to educate the people about the meaning of sovereignty and the forms it might take, such as independence or Native American status. Act 140, An Act Relating to the Hawaiian Sovereignty Elections Council, 1996 Hawaiian Session Laws 396, in LEXIS through all of the 1996 legislation.[5] Finally, the state government provided funding for a referendum—commonly referred to as "the plebiscite" among native Hawaiians—on the question of whether the Hawaiian people should elect delegates to propose a native Hawaiian government. *Id.*

Not everyone in favor of native Hawaiian sovereignty was in favor of the plebiscite. Two lawsuits were consolidated in the United States District Court for the District of Hawaii to enjoin the plebiscite from counting the ballots. *Rice v. Cayetano,* No. Civ. 96-00390 DAE, WESTLAW 1996, p. 88343, at *4, District Court of Hawaii, September 6, 1996.[6] One action was by a group claiming to represent native Hawaiian interests and arguing that a plebiscite sponsored by the state government would interfere with the right to petition the federal government for sovereignty. *Rice v. Cayetano,* No. Civ. 96-00390 DAE, WESTLAW 1996, p. 88343, at *8, District Court of Hawaii, September 6, 1996.[7] The second was brought by an individual on the ground that state dollars should not be allowed to fund a plebiscite in which only native Hawaiians could vote. *Rice v. Cayetano,* No. Civ. 96-00390 DAE, WESTLAW 1996, p. 88343, at *9, District Court of Hawaii, September 6, 1996.[8] The district court denied the injunction in both instances. *Rice.*[9] The plaintiffs have been granted

leave to appeal, and the legal issues remain unresolved.

1. _____

_____

Rule(s) _____

_____

2. _____

_____

Rule(s) _____

_____

3. _____

_____

Rule(s) _____

_____

4. _____

_____

Rule(s) _____

_____

5. _____

_____

Rule(s) _____

_____

6. _____

_____

Rule(s) _____

_____

7. _____

_____

Rule(s) _____

_____

8. _____

_____

Rule(s) _____

_____

9. _____

_____

Rule(s) _____

_____

PART V
SHORT CITATION FORMS

In the sample exercise in the introduction to the Citation Placement and Frequency Exercises, you met the citation form *id*. *Id*. is a **short citation form** often called a **short cite**. In this chapter you will learn how to use short citation forms.

Short citation forms are used in a document once you have cited a particular authority and wish to cite to it again. Since you have already given the reader all the important information the citation must contain the first time you cited the authority, you only need remind the reader that you have done so. Here are some examples:

Example 1:

In 1905, the state of Indiana prohibited the sale, manufacture, and possession of cigarettes. Ind. Code Ann. § 2216 (Michie 1905). The statute, however, specifically exempted cigarettes that only passed through the state. *Id*.

The short form citation provides the source of the exception to the prohibition, which is the statute already cited; *Id*. means that the citation is the same as the previous one. **Rule 4.1** contains guidelines for the use of *Id*.

Example 2:

In the case of *Palsgraf v. Long Island R.R. Co.,* 248 N.Y. 339, 162 N.E. 99 (1922), Justice Cardozo gave the classical definition of proximate cause. He wrote that "the risk reasonably to be perceived defined the duty to be obeyed, and risk imports relation; it is risk to another or to others within the range of apprehension ...." *Id*. at 343, 162 N.E. at 100.

This short citation form tells the reader that the quotation comes from Justice Cardozo's opinion in *Palsgraf v. Long Island R.R. Co.* Since you are quoting from the opinion and not referring to it again in general, you must add the page number upon which the quotation appears. **Rule 4.1** and **P.4** shows you how to modify the use of *Id*. to include such additional information.

Id. is only one type of short citation. There are a variety of ways to shorten the citation forms of authorities you have fully cited to once in a document. Each type of authority has its own short citation form, depending on where and when in your document you are re-referring to the authority. You will find a rule about short citation forms towards the end of many rules in the Bluebook. For example, the short form rule for statutes is in **Rule 12.9**, the last rule in **Rule 12** which covers the citation of statutes. The basic short citation form for all authorities can be found in **Rule 4** and in **P.4**.

The following two exercises will help you learn how to use short citation forms. The first exercise concentrates on the forms themselves, and the second on the placement of short citation forms as well as their forms.

Citation Exercise #6

In this exercise, you will be given a full citation. You will have to choose the proper short citation based on the clues available.

1. You wish to cite to *Nutrilab, Inc. v. Schweicker,* 713 F.2d 335 (7th Cir. 1983), again without having cited to any other authorities in the interim. The proper short citation form is:

   a. Id

   b. *Id.*

   c. *Supra.*

2. You wish to cite to page 337 of *Nutrilab, Inc. v. Schweicker,* 713 F.2d 335 (7th Cir. 1983). You have already cited this case, but after you cited to the case, you cited to a number of other authorities. The proper citation form is:

   a. *Nutrilab, Inc. v. Schweicker,* 713 F.2d at 337.

   b. *Nutrilab, Inc. v. Schweicker, supra,* at 337.

   c. *Nutrilab, Inc. v. Schweicker,* 713 at 337.

3. In the very next sentence, you quote from page 338 of *Nutrilab, Inc. v. Schweicker,* 713 F.2d 335 (7th Cir. 1983). There are no intervening citations. The proper short citation form is:

   a. *Id.,* 713 F.2d at 338.

   b. *Id.*

   c. *Id.* at 338.

4. You have just cited *Inter City Motor Sales v. Szymanski,* 42 Mich. App. 112, 201 N.W.2d 378 (1972). You wish to quote in the very next sentence, with no intervening citations to other authorities, some text from page 115 of the Michigan Appellate reporter which also appears on page 379 of the Northwest Second reporter. The proper short citation form is:

   a. 42 Mich. App. 112, at page 115, 201 N.W.2d 378, at page 379.

   b. *Id.* at 115, 201 N.W.2d at 379.

   c. *Id.* at pages 115 and 379.

5. You cited to John Alan Appleman, *Insurance Law and Practice* §
    9746 (1981). You wish to cite later in your document, after having
    cited to several intervening authorities, to § 9751 of the same trea-
    tise. The proper citation form is:

    a.   *Id.* at § 9751.

    b.   Appleman on Insurance, at § 9751.

    c.   Appleman, *supra,* at § 9751.

6. You wish to cite to page 56 of Richard B. Collins, *Economic Union as
    a Constitutional Value*, 63 N.Y.U. L. Rev. 43 (1988), again after citing
    to six other authorities in the interim. The proper short citation
    form is:

    a.   Collins, *supra,* at 56.

    b.   Collins at 56.

    c.   Richard B. Collins, *Economic Union as a Constitutional Value,*
         63 N.Y.U. L. Rev. at 56 (1988).

7. You are writing a memorandum involving only N.Y. Civ. Rights Law
    § 50 (McKinney 1990) as statutory authority. After the first time you
    cite fully to this statute, the proper short citation form, assuming
    there are intervening citations to other authorities, is:

    a.   N.Y.C.R. § 50.

    b.   § 50.

    c.   McKinney § 50.

Citation Exercise #7

This exercise contains excerpts from a discussion section of an interoffice memorandum of law, a judicial opinion and a statute. The memorandum relies on the judicial opinion and statute to make its argument; however, it contains no citations. You must put the citations in the appropriate places in the memorandum, much as you did in the Citation Placement Exercise in Part II. You will have to use full and short citation forms. Please use parallel citations, even though they are not required since this document is not being submitted to a state court, so that you can have practice using them. The exercise is triple-spaced to provide you room to insert the appropriate citations.

Memorandum

Excerpt from Discussion:

The New Jersey Department of Motor Vehicles (hereinafter "DMV"),

the employer of our client, Mr. James Stuart, may have failed to provide

Mr. Stuart with a safe place to work pursuant to New Jersey law by not

ensuring that Mr. Stuart had a smoke-free environment in which to work.

In order to protect the health, welfare and comfort of non-smoking

employees, New Jersey legislation forbids smoking in government build-

ings such as the one in which Mr. Stuart works. Therefore, the DMV can-

not argue that it need not accommodate Mr. Stuart's desire for a

smoke-free working environment at all. The legislation, however, does not

prohibit smoking in each and every part of the building; it only requires

that the supervisor of each government unit establish written rules to fairly accommodate the needs of smoking and non-smoking employees. Pursuant to this statute, Mr. Stuart's supervisor established rules prohibiting smoking in the public areas of the DMV, such as the hallways and lobbies, but permitted smoking in private offices. Mr. Stuart has his own office in which he does not smoke. He has not complained of anyone smoking in the hallways outside his office, but of his colleagues' smoking in adjacent offices because the smoke circulates through a common ventilation system. Mr. Stuart, therefore, might not be able to obtain relief under the New Jersey no smoking law.

Mr. Stuart, however, might be able to obtain relief under New Jersey common law. Prior to the New Jersey legislature's enactment of its no smoking law, a New Jersey court held that an employer has a general duty to provide a safe place to work which requires that smoking be forbidden in the work area. Therefore, whether Mr. Stuart can successfully state a common law cause of action depends in large part on whether a court will view the New Jersey legislation as overturning the holding of the case with respect to the presence of tobacco smoke.

Assuming that a court will find that a common law cause of action exists, the next issue that Mr. Stuart must confront is whether the mere presence of tobacco smoke constitutes a hazardous working condition as understood by the *Shimp* court. If the presence of tobacco smoke makes a workplace unsafe, then Mr. Stuart probably has a cause of action. The *Shimp* case addressed this issue in great detail and found that tobacco smoke did indeed create a hazardous work situation.

The facts of Mr. Stuart's case closely parallel those of *Shimp*. Both worked in offices and both were highly allergic to the cigarette smoke which permeated the atmosphere of the workplace. However, the *Shimp* plaintiff occupied a desk in a large work area and not in a separate office. Thus, the DMV may argue that it has done all it needs to do under the law to accommodate Mr. Stuart by providing him with a private office under the rules it established pursuant to the New Jersey legislation. At the same time, however, while the *Shimp* court did not address the question of tobacco smoke circulating from one office to another, it did emphasize that, although the employer attempted to alleviate the plaintiff's problem, it had not done enough to escape liability since the plaintiff continued to suffer.

Mr. Stuart may also use the public policy expressed in the New Jersey legislation to buttress an argument that New Jersey finds that tobacco smoke creates a hazardous working situation. The statute expressly

states that "tobacco smoke is . . . a substantial health hazard to a smaller

segment of the nonsmoking public."

Excerpts from Statutes

Title 26. Health and Vital Statistics
Chapter 3D. Smoking in Public Places
Government Buildings

N.J. Rev. Stat. § 26:3D-46 (1992)

Legislative findings and declarations

The legislature finds and declares that the resolution of the conflict between the right of the smoker to smoke and the right of the nonsmoker to breathe clean air involves a determination of when and where, rather than whether, a smoker may legally smoke. It is not the public policy of this State to deny anyone the right to smoke. However, the Legislature finds that in those government buildings affected by this act the right of the nonsmoker to breathe clean air should supersede the right of the smoker to smoke. In addition to the deleterious effects upon smokers, tobacco smoke is (1) at least an annoyance and a nuisance to a substantial percentage of the nonsmoking public, and (2) a substantial health hazard to a smaller segment of the nonsmoking public. The purpose of this act, therefore, is to protect the interest of nonsmokers in government buildings and allow smokers the right to smoke in designated areas in government buildings.

N.J. Rev. Stat. § 26:3D-48 (1992)

Establishing of written rules governing smoking in government buildings; notice and hearing

a. (1) Except for areas occupied by the Legislature, its committees and personnel, the supervisor of each unit of government located in a government building shall establish written rules governing smoking in the building or that portion of the building for which the supervisor is responsible. The rules shall contain a written policy and procedure to protect the health, welfare and comfort of employees from the detrimental effects of tobacco smoke which policy shall include designated nonsmoking areas but may include designated smoking areas. Nothing in this act shall prevent any rule, regulation or procedure, which is not contrary to the provisions of this act, from being established by an employer or negotiated as a term or condition of any agreement or contract of employment. Employees shall be provided with a copy of the written rules upon request.

Excerpt from Judicial Opinion

145 N.J. Super. 516
368 A.2d 408
Donna M. SHIMP, Plaintiff

v.

NEW JERSEY BELL TELEPHONE
COMPANY, Defendant.

Superior Court of New Jersey,
Chancery Division.

Dec. 20, 1976.

[145 N.J. 516-520, 368 A.2d 408-409]

[145 N.J. Super. 520, 368 A.2d 409] GRUCCIO, J.S.C.

This case involves a matter of first impression in this State: whether a nonsmoking employee is denied a safe working environment and entitled to injunctive relief when forced by proximity to smoking employees to involuntarily inhale "second hand" cigarette smoke.

Plaintiff seeks to have cigarette smoking enjoined in the area where she works. She alleges that her employer, defendant N.J. Bell Telephone Co., is causing her to work in an unsafe environment by refusing to enact a ban against smoking in the office where she works. The company allows other employees to smoke while on the job at desks situated in the same work **[368 A.2d 410]** area as that of the plaintiff. Plaintiff contends that the passive inhalation of smoke and the gaseous by-products of burning tobacco is deleterious to her health. Therefore her employer, by permitting employees to smoke in the work area, is allowing an unsafe condition to exist. The present action is a suit to enjoin these allegedly unsafe conditions, thereby restoring to plaintiff a healthy environment in which to work.

[145 N.J. Super. 521, 368 A.2d 410]

. . . Plaintiff's affidavit clearly outlines a legitimate grievance based upon a genuine health problem. She is allergic to cigarette smoke. Mere passive inhalation causes a severe allergic reaction which has forced her to leave work physically ill on numerous occasions. . . .

Plaintiff sought to alleviate her intolerable working situation through the use of grievance mechanisms established by collective bargaining between defendant employer and her union. That action, together with other efforts of plaintiff and her physician, resulted in the installation of an exhaust fan in the vicinity of her work area. This attempted solution has proven unsuccessful because the fan was not kept in continuous operation. The other employees complained of cold drafts due to the fan's operation, and compromises involving operation at set intervals have proven ineffective to prevent the onset of plaintiff's symptoms in the presence of smoking coemployees. . . .

It is clearly the law in this State that an employee has a right to work in a safe environment. An employer is under an affirmative duty to provide a work area that is free from unsafe conditions. *McDonald v. Standard Oil Co.*, 69 N.J.L. 445, 55 A. 289 (E. & A. 1903). . . . This right to safe and healthful working conditions is protected not only by the duty imposed by common law upon employers, **[145 N.J. Super. 522]** but has also been the subject of federal legislation. In 1970 Congress enacted the Occupational Safety and Health Act (OSHA), 29 U.S.C.A. § 651-78, which expresses a policy of prevention of occupational hazards. The act authorizes the Secretary of Labor to set mandatory occupational safety and health standards in order to assure safe and healthful working conditions. 29 U.S.C.A. § 651. Under the general duty clause, 29 U.S.C.A. § 654(a)(1), Congress imposed upon the employer a duty to eliminate all foreseeable and preventable hazards. *Cal. Stevedore & Ballast Co. v. O.S.H.R.C.*, 517 F.2d 986, 988 (9 Cir. 1975). . . . OSHA in no way preempted the field of occupational safety. Specifically, **[368 A.2d 411]** 29 U.S.C.A. § 653(b)(4) recognizes concurrent state power to act either legislatively or judicially under the common law with regard to occupational safety. . . .

[145 N.J. Super. 522-525, 368 A.2d. 411-413]

[145 N.J. Super 525, 368 A.2d 413] Since plaintiff has a common law right to a safe working environment, the issue remains whether the work area here **[145 N.J. Super. 526]** is unsafe due to a preventable hazard which I may enjoin. There can be no doubt that the by-products of burning tobacco are toxic and dangerous to the health of smokers and nonsmokers generally and to this plaintiff in particular.

In 1965 Congress officially recognized the dangerous nature of cigarette smoke and declared a national policy to warn the public of the danger and to discourage cigarette smoking. . . .

[145 N.J. Super. 527, 368 A.2d 414] The HEW report for 1975, *The Health Consequences of Smoking*, and the Surgeon General's report by the same title for 1972 reveal distressing new evidence in the continuing investigation of the toxic nature of cigarette smoke. The reports indicate that the mere presence of cigarette smoke in the air pollutes it, changing carbon monoxide levels and effectively making involuntary smokers of all who breathe the air. . . .

[**145 N.J. Super. 528**] The Surgeon General's findings are supported strongly by the evidence which has been presented to me. . . . Dr. Wilbert S. Aronow, a Cardiologist who is Chief of Cardiovascular Research at the University of California at Irvine, has submitted with his affidavit the result of extensive research and testimony collected in a paper entitled "The Effect of [**368 A.2d 415**] Passive Smoking on the Cardiovascular and Respiratory Systems." In that paper Mr. Aronow concludes that passive smoking not only aggravates the condition of persons with cardiovascular or pulmonary disease, but also may lead to increased respiratory and other symptoms in *nonallergic* patients sensitive to tobacco. . . .

[**145 N.J. Super. 528-530, 368 A.2d 415-416**]

[**145 N.J. Super. 530**] The evidence is clear and overwhelming. Cigarette smoke contaminates and pollutes the air, creating a health hazard not merely to the smoker but to all those around her who must rely upon the same air supply. The right of an individual to risk his or her own health does not include the right to jeopardize the health of those who must remain around him or her in order to properly perform the duties of [**145 N.J. Super. 531**] their jobs. The portion of the population which is especially sensitive to cigarette smoke is so significant that it is reasonable to expect an employer to foresee health consequences and to impose upon [**368 A.2d 416**] him a duty to abate the hazard which causes the discomfort. . . .

In determining the extent to which smoking must be restricted the rights and interests of smoking and nonsmoking employees alike must be considered. The employees' rights to a safe working environment make it clear that smoking must be forbidden in the work area. The employee who desires to smoke on his own time, during coffee breaks and lunch hours, should have a reasonably accessible area in which to smoke. . . . Such a rule imposes no hardship upon defendant New Jersey Bell Telephone Company. The company already has in effect a rule that cigarettes may not be smoked around the telephone equipment. . . .

Accordingly, I order defendant New Jersey Bell Telephone Company to provide safe working conditions for plaintiff by restricting the smoking of employees to the nonwork areas presently used as a lunchroom. No smoking shall be permitted in the offices or adjacent customer service area.

It is so ordered.

PART VI
PUTTING IT ALL TOGETHER

Before we try to put it all together, you should become more familiar with the use of signals. You were first introduced to signals in Part II. Because signals are sophisticated writing and citation tools and because their use is best demonstrated in a longer document (although they can be used in documents of any size—and should be when required), we have waited until you have mastered some of the more basic elements of citations before giving a fuller explanation of how signals work.

The sixteenth edition of the Bluebook eliminated or modified rules regarding signals present in previous editions of the Bluebook and generally accepted by the legal community. Because we disagree with these changes, we are including here definitions that we believe will make the legal analysis in your writing more precise and clear. This is just a brief introduction to the use of signals. You will get a better sense of how they are used in the "Snow White" and "Caesar" exercises that follow.

Note: Use **Rule 1.2** of the sixteenth edition of the Bluebook for typographical conventions only. Use **Rule 1.3** for general order of signals and **Rule 1.4** for the order of authorities within a signal.

The Signals:

1. *No Signal.* The total lack of a signal before a citation offers the strongest support for the legal proposition you are making; the authority you cite is on all fours. "No signal" is also used when the legal proposition contains a quote from the authority cited.

The jury found that the prince did say, "Rapunzel, Rapunzel, let down your hair." *Rapunzel v. Witch,* 2 Grimm 125, 126 (1814).

2. *E.g.,* (for example). This signal can be combined with any other signal. Use it when you have lots of authority for the legal proposition but do not want to boggle the reader's mind.

Fairy tales cannot end happily for all parties involved. *E.g., White v. Rose,* 1 Grimm 25 (1812); *Giant v. Jack,* 3 Beanstalk 172 (1654).

3. *Accord.* This signal is similar to "no signal" but is used when your text incorporates a citation and you wish to add additional authority, espectally from a different, jurisdiction, in a citation sentence.

In *White v. Rose,* 1 Grimm 25 (1812), the court concluded that fairy tales cannot end happily for all parties involved. *Accord Giant v. Jack,* 3 Beanstalk 172 (1654).

4. *See.* This citation supports your legal proposition on all threes.

Fairy tale courts do not consider the role of fairy wishes as much as they could. *See In re: Beauty v. Charming,* 4 Grimm 97 (1815).

5.   *See also.* Use *see also* when you are introducing a citation that provides additional support that is on all threes. It is best when used with an explanatory parenthetical.
   Rule 1.5, Rule 10.6 and Rule 12.7 of the Bluebook contain guidelines for writing explanatory parentheticals (also called parenthetical information).[1]
   See also Stepsisters v. Cinderella, 2 Grimm 72 (1813) (holding that stepsisters could not demand that Cinderella appoint them as ladies-in-waiting).

6.   *Cf.* (from the Latin *conferre,* to compare). Use this signal when the cited authority supports your proposition on all two and a half. An explanatory parenthetical is highly recommended.
   Politically correct fairy tales often miss the point. *Cf.* James Finn Garner, *Politically Correct Bedtime Stories* (1994) (exploring consequences of attaching contemporary mores to ancient cases).

7.   *Compare* (citation) *with* (citation). Use this signal when only a comparison of authorities will support your proposition. The use of this signal usually indicates that you have not been able to find authority on all fours or all threes. This signal demands explanatory parentheticals.
   Fairy tale courts may be biased against witches. *Compare Witch's Estate v. Hansel,* 3 Grimm 47 (1815) (describing the witch as a cannibal and upholding the actions of the defendants throwing her into a hot oven), *with Rapunzel v. Witch,* 2 Grimm 125 (1814) (holding defendant liable for false imprisonment).

8.   *See generally.* Use this signal when the authority you cite contains general background information. *See also* may sometimes be used the same way.
   The laws of the courts of Fairy Tale go back thousands of years. *See generally* Brothers Grimm, *Fairy Tale Jurisprudence* § 1 (1815).

9.   *Contra.* This is the opposite of "no signal." Use it when you must cite authority that directly contradicts your proposition. *Contra* is used in a manner analogous to *accord* when you already have a citation to support your proposition but must cite one contradicting it as well. (Note: This signal does not appear in the sixteenth editon of the Bluebook. You can find it in the fifteenth and previous editions.)

---

   [1] **Rule 1.5** states that an explanatory parenthetical which describes what a case stands for begins with a present participle (---ing). In general, this is a good way to begin; however, you may see citations with parentheticals that begin with some other part of speech or phrase "where court held, etc." With experience, you will learn how best to make an explanatory parenthetical "explain." For now, follow the Bluebook guidelines.

Fairy tales do not end happily for all parties involved. *Stepsisters v. Cinderella*, 2 Grimm 72 (1813). *Contra Cindrella II v. Stepsisters,* 1 Perrault 2d 72 (1780).

10.   *But see.* This signal is the opposite of *see* and, like *contra*, used when you must point out authority that may contradict your proposition. It is less strong than *contra* and is used more often.

The principle guiding the Fairy tale courts seems to be stated as: "Be careful what you wish for; you may get it." *Aladdin v. Genie*, 1 Scheherezade 1001 (1885). *But see Rapunzel v. Witch*, 2 Grimm 125 (1814).

11.   *But cf.* This signal is the opposite of *cf.* It is less strong than *but see.*

12.   There is no signal that is the opposite of *compare* (citation) *with* (citation).

The Exercises:

The following exercises test your knowledge of all of the basic rules of legal citation. On the sheets provided, please correct each shadowed citation; for each correction made, note the governing rule(s).

Let us look at the first citation (#1) to the second exercise, the "Caesar" Citation Exercise, as an example.

See New York Pen. L. sec. 150.20 (McKinney 1988).

On your answer sheet, your answer would look like this:

#1   Corrected Citation:
See N.Y. Penal Law § 150.20 (McKinney 1988).
Rule(s):
T.1, New York; Rule 6.2(b).

You should note three things about the "Snow White" and "Caesar" citation exercises. First, the exercises are in the form of a sample judicial opinion. You may note from your case law readings that citations in judicial opinions are different from those that you are required to write. The reason for this is that a court may have its own rules of citation different from those in the Bluebook. Thus, you should consult the court for its citation rules before submitting a document to that particular court. For purposes of this exercise, this particular court follows the rules of the Bluebook; in regard to parallel citations, it requires parallel citations.

Second, the "Caesar" exercise contains citations to New York legislative history materials with which you are probably not familiar. In citing to the legislative history or other materials particular to a given jurisdiction, you may want to see if the particular state has a guide to citing its own materials in lieu of the Bluebook because the Bluebook may not be complete for each state. For example, in New York, St. John's University Law Review publishes a guide to citations for New York materials called the *New York Rules of Citation*. It is very well-written, well-organized and more comprehensive than the Bluebook.

Third, the format for exercise #8 and #9 differs from that of previous exercises. The citations which contain errors are preceded by a number with a number sign (#) and are shaded *e.g.*, #1 400 Misc. 2d 1000 #2 900 N.Y. Supp. 2d 947 #3 (2010). The superscripted numbers refer to footnotes.

We have used the *New York Rules of Citation* to write the citations for the legislative material in the "Caesar" exercise. *Therefore, you should not correct these citations according to the Bluebook rules governing legislative history materials.* You may find other Bluebook errors, and, where applicable, you should correct them.

"Snow White" Citation Exercise #8

White v. Stepmother,
#1 400 Misc. 2d 1000 #2 900 N.Y.Supp.2d947
3 (2010).

In this case, one of first impression to this #4 court, the plaintiff has brought suit against the defendant on the theory of wrongful death, claiming that the defendant did cause the plaintiff's death by intentionally feeding her an apple laced with poison. The plaintiff is alive today it seems thanks to the scientifically advanced mouth-to-mouth resuscitation efforts of one Mr. Prince. (This technique is characterized as "The Kiss.")

The issue is whether an individual can be liable for the death of a presently living person.

The plaintiff, Ms. Snow White,[1] has alleged that The Wicked Stepmother had long been jealous of her and had attempted, while aided and abetted by Mr. Woodman, in the past to "cut her heart out." #5 (Record, p. 10.)[2] While Snow White escaped that attempt on her life, she was not so fortunate as to escape the September 9, 2009 murder attempt.

---

[1] While Ms. White has married Mr. Prince, she has continued to use her professional name, Snow White.

[2] Snow White had previously named Mr. Woodman as defendant in a reckless endangerment complaint and in a civil suit claiming failure to rescue. #6 Accord #7 *People of New York v. Woodman*, No. 25-355 (#8 S.Ct.N.Y. filed #9 December 9, 2009, #10 withdrawn Jan. 30, 2010; *White v. Woodman*, No. 25-330 (#8 S.Ct.N.Y. filed Dec. 1, 2009), #10 withdrawn Jan. 30, 2010.

Initially, this court would note that this matter is ripe for review, given the ever-changing state of modern medicine and the healing arts. #11 See, *Hook v. Alligator*, #12 392 N.Y. 2d 21, 550 N.E.2d 420, #13 885 N.Y.S.2d 227 (#14 Court of Appeals agreeing to address pain and suffering allegation of plaintiff who had been temporarily swallowed and then regurgitated by the defendant).

The relevant facts are as follows. On September 9, 2009, The Wicked Stepmother, disguised as an old beggar woman, appeared at the back door of Snow White's residence in the Catskills.[3] Snow White was alone at the time. She let the woman in and bought an apple from her. Immediately upon eating a few bites of the apple, Snow White fell into a coma. Snow White's claim is that she was not in a coma, but was dead at that time, and that, many months later, her future husband administered the kiss that brought her back to life.

There is ample evidence as to the identity of the perpetrator. Indeed, Snow White's seven roommates, who were returning from work at the time, saw the old woman drop her basket of apples as she fled their home. And while they thought that the old woman had accidentally fallen to her death during the chase, she had actually only fallen from a ledge into a mudhole. She was later discovered there and detained by an irate pig owner, one Farmer McDonald.

---

[3]   During this period of her life, Snow White had been living with seven miners.

While there is no case directly on point in New York, in 2008, the California Supreme Court dealt with a similar legal scenario. In *Beauty v. Maleficent*, #15 709 P.2d 45, #16 495 Cal.3d 890, #17 655 Cal.Rptr. 69, (2008), the court held that a wrongful death action would lie where pricking her finger on a poison-laden spinning wheel needle caused a young woman to remain completely inert for one hundred years. The court reasoned that #18 ". . . only in fairy tales do people generally live beyond one hundred years; therefore, to take away that natural life span is to 'kill' a person." #19 Id. at 70, 709 P.2d at 47, 495 Cal. 3d at 892. Such reasoning cannot be decisive in the case at bar since Snow White remained inert for only a few months, far short of the "average life span" criterion that the *Maleficent* court used.

20

More on point is the case of #21 *The Prince*[4] *AKA "The Beast"* #22 *v. Wicked Witch* 549 N.W.2d 709 #23 (2008). In that case, the defendant's malicious actions resulted in the plaintiff's suffering a deforming illness, which illness rendered him beast-like in appearance and manner for several years. In deciding the intentional tort action in favor of the plaintiff, the court held that, while his injuries were not the usual (e.g., broken bones, concussions, etc.), they were certainly real. The court added, "It is not the length of time that the affliction lasts which should be the key con-

---

[4] This Prince is not the same Prince who developed "The Kiss" and later married Snow White.

sideration; rather, a court should look to the *effect* of the affliction during its tenure." #24 *The Prince*, at 711 #25; emphasis added.

We agree with the reasoning in *The Prince*. For a three-month period, Snow White was functionally dead. Had a miracle cure such as "The Kiss" not been found, she would still be in a permanent state of inertia. This case cannot benefit from the learned decisions handed down in cases involving the removal of life-support systems from long-term coma patients. #26 (*Roberts v.* #27 *The Glendale* #28 *Hospital,* 650 N.J. Super. 5, 952 A.2d 67 (Super. Ct. App. Div. #29 1999), *Barnes v. Lewis,* 789 N.J. 44, 509 A.2d 77 (2003). Neither the giving, nor the taking away, of normally administered medical aid would have affected Snow White. 30

We, therefore, find the defendant, The Wicked Stepmother, guilty of wrongful death. It is no longer true, at least in this jurisdiction, that dead men (and women) tell no tales.

Answers (Citation Exercise #7)

#1. Corrected Citation:

_____

_____

Rule(s): _____

_____

_____

#2. Corrected Citation:

_____

_____

Rule(s): _____

_____

_____

#3. Corrected Citation:

_____

_____

Rule(s): _____

_____

_____

#4. Corrected Citation:

_____

_____

Rule(s): _____

_____

_____

#5. Corrected Citation:

_____

_____

Rule(s): _____

_____

_____

#6   Corrected Citation:

_____

_____

Rule(s): _____

_____

_____

#7. Corrected Citation:

_____

_____

Rule(s): _____

_____

_____

#8. Corrected Citation:

_____

_____

Rule(s): _____

_____

_____

#9. Corrected Citation:

_____

_____

Rule(s): _____

_____

_____

#10. Corrected Citation:

_____

_____

Rule(s):   _____

_____

_____

#11. Corrected Citation:

_____

_____

Rule(s):   _____

_____

_____

#12. Corrected Citation:

_____

_____

Rule(s):   _____

_____

_____

#13. Corrected Citation:

_____

_____

Rule(s):   _____

_____

_____

#14. Corrected Citation:

_____

_____

Rule(s):   _____

_____

_____

#15. Corrected Citation:

_____

_____

Rule(s): _____

_____

_____

#16. Corrected Citation:

_____

_____

Rule(s): _____

_____

_____

#17. Corrected Citation:

_____

_____

Rule(s): _____

_____

_____

#18. Corrected Citation:

_____

_____

Rule(s): _____

_____

_____

#19. Corrected Citation:

_____

_____

Rule(s): _____

_____

_____

#20. Corrected Citation:

_____

_____

Rule(s): _____

_____

_____

#21. Corrected Citation:

_____

_____

Rule(s): _____

_____

_____

#22. Corrected Citation:

_____

_____

Rule(s): _____

_____

_____

#23. Corrected Citation:

_____

_____

Rule(s): _____

_____

_____

#24. Corrected Citation:

_____

_____

Rule(s): _____

_____

_____

#25. Corrected Citation:

_____

_____

Rule(s): _____

_____

_____

#26. Corrected Citation:

_____

_____

Rule(s): _____

_____

_____

#27. Corrected Citation:

_____

_____

Rule(s): _____

_____

_____

#28. Corrected Citation:

_____

_____

Rule(s): _____

_____

_____

#29. Corrected Citation:

_____

_____

Rule(s): _____

_____

_____

#30. Corrected Citation:

_____

_____

Rule(s): _____

_____

_____

"Caesar" Citation Exercise #9

Rex v. Caesar,
130 Misc. 2d 80, 520 N.Y.S.2d 60 (Sup. Ct. N.Y. County 1988).

Cleopatra owned a beautiful dog named "Roman Nose." On July 27, 1991, Julius Caesar ("Caesar") and Marc Antony ("Antony") were convicted in New York of arson in the first degree for setting fire to Roman Nose's doghouse. #1 *See* New York Pen. L. sec. 150.20 (McKinney 1988). One issue before this Court is whether Roman Nose's doghouse is a "building" within the meaning of #2 § 150.00 of the New York Penal Law. #3 *See* N.Y. Penal Law § 150.00(1) (McKinney 1988). A second issue before this Court is whether the device the defendants used to set fire to the doghouse, a "Molotov cocktail," is an "incendiary device" within the meaning of section 150.20. *See id.* § 150.20(2). On the weight of the authority of the recent decision of the New York Court of Appeals in #4 *Agrippina v. Nero*, 70 N.Y.2d 165, 500 N.Y.S.2d 118, 520 N.E.2d 85 (1988), this Court finds that "historical figures" and their feline, canine and bovine companions are "persons" within the meaning of section 150.20. #5 *Agrippina v. Nero*, 70 N.Y.2d at 168, 500 N.Y.S.2d at 122 (holding that "historical figures" are "persons" who may sue or be sued in New York for intentional torts).

The testimony at trial established the following facts. On April 1, 1991, at the instigation of Cleopatra, Roman Nose, a renowned practical joker, took Caesar's favorite tunic from a clothesline where Caesar had set it out to dry.[1] An unidentified cat allegedly stole the tunic from Roman Nose while Roman Nose was sleeping. The tunic was never recovered. (R. at 135.)

When Cleopatra told Caesar what Roman Nose had done, Caesar became enraged and told Cleopatra, in front of a roomful of witnesses, "I will have my revenge. You are to me as Delilah was to Samson, for you and your dog have stolen the source of my strength, my prowess and my wisdom." #6 *See* Judges 16, 14-20. (R. at 138-39.)

Later that evening, Caesar and Antony hid behind Roman Nose's doghouse. Caesar looked in the window and saw Roman Nose inside clearing his dinner dishes. Roman Nose did this each night before he went to Cleopatra's house where he slept for the night. While Caesar held the bottle, Antony lit the wick of a "Molotov cocktail." Antony then hurled the bottle at Roman Nose's doghouse. Witnesses testified that, as they ran from the flaming doghouse, Caesar and Antony cried, "Burn, Delilah, burn." Roman Nose escaped physical injury, but the doghouse was

---

[1] Roman Nose knew that this particular tunic was Caesar's favorite, for it was the tunic Caesar wore when he met Cleopatra and the tunic Caesar always wore when he went into battle. Roman Nose has played numerous practical jokes on Caesar involving the "theft" of Caesar's tunic or sandals. These practical jokes have given rise to two civil actions. #7 *See* Caesar v. Nose, 120 Misc. 2d 342, 507 N.Y.S.2d 835 (N.Y. Civ. Ct. 1985) (holding that Roman Nose was not liable for conversion because Roman Nose did not "wrongfully acquire" posession of tunic); Caesar v. Nose, 100 A.D.2d 650, 503 N.Y.S.2d 621 (4th Dep't 1985) (holding that Caesar did not establish that Roman Nose had sufficient intent to exercise "dominion" or "control" over sandals).

destroyed. At trial, an arson expert identified charred scraps of paper found near the doghouse to be from one of Antony's scrolls.[2] #8 Transcript at 140-55.

Doghouse As "Building"

Section 150.20(1) of the New York Penal Law provides in pertinent part:

> A person is guilty of arson in the first degree when he intentionally damages a building . . . by causing an explosion or fire and when (a) such explosion or fire is caused by an incendiary device propelled, thrown or placed inside or near such building . . .; and when (b) another person who is not a participant in the crime is present in such building at the time; and (c) the defendant knows that fact or the circumstances are such as to render the presence of such person therein a reasonable possibility.

#9   § 150.20(1).

Section 150.00 defines the term "building" to include, "in addition to its ordinary meaning, . . . any structure, . . . used for overnight lodging of persons." *Id.* § 150.00(1). The recent case, *Rex v. Calf*, 125 A.D.2d 63, 515 N.Y.S.2d 719 (3d Dep't), *aff'd,* 70 N.Y.2d 10, 509 N.E.2d 233, 517 N.Y.S.2d 755 (1987), demonstrates that a doghouse should not be included in the "ordinary meaning" of the term "building." In #10 *Calf, supra*, the Third Department found that a "golden calf" house is not a "building" within the

---

[2] Royal proclamations were made on scrolls, which were made of a special papyrus. Each Roman official of high rank had his own identifiable scrolls made of the special papyrus.

"ordinary meaning" of section 150.20. #11 *Id.* at 66, 515 N.Y.S.2d at 722, *aff'd,* 70 N.Y.2d 10, 509 N.E.2d 233, 517 N.Y.S.2d 755 (1987). The court argued that "a golden calf house is not the first thing that comes to mind when one thinks of a 'building.'" *Id.* at 68, 515 N.Y.S.2d at 726; #12 *cf. Rex v. Beelzebub,* 117 Misc. 2d 514, 517, 363 N.Y.S.2d 970, 975 (Sup. Ct. Albany County 1976) (holding "ark" used to transport animals during flood not "building" within "ordinary meaning" of section 150.20); *Rex v. Abaddon,* 112 A.D.2d 625, 476 N.Y.S.2d 39 (2d Dep't 1984), *affirmed,* 50 N.Y.2d 219, 500 N.E.2d 75, 478 N.Y.S.2d 80 (1984) (same).

We also find that Roman Nose's doghouse is not a "structure used for overnight lodging" under section 150.20. *See* § 150.00(1). Although this issue is one of first impression in this state, courts in other jurisdictions have found that a doghouse that a dog does not sleep in at night is not a "structure used for overnight lodging" under the state's arson statute. #13 *See, e.g., Rex v. Lucius,* 210 S.W. 2d 68, 70 (1966) (reversing on appeal arson conviction of Lucius and Fulvia for setting fire to Octavian's dog's doghouse); *State of Arkansas v. Octavian,* 75 Ark. 903, 905, 350 S.W.2d 821 (1984) (reversing on appeal Octavian's conviction of arson of Marc Antony's dog's doghouse).

Sections 140.20 and 140.25 of the Penal Law define burglary in the second and third degrees in part as the "unlawful[ ] [remaining] in a 'building' with the intent to commit a crime therein." #14 N.Y. Penal

Law §§ 140.20-140.25 (1988). Section 140.00 of the Penal Law defines "building" as including "in addition to its ordinary meaning, . . . any structure . . . used for overnight lodging of persons." *Id.* § 140.00(2). Cases construing New York's burglary statutes demonstrate that the term "building" does not include a doghouse if the dog does not use the doghouse at night. #15 *See, e.g., Rex v. Caligula,* 108 Misc.2d 89, 91, 402 N.Y.S. 2d 743, 747 (Sup.Ct. Westchester County 1980) (exonerating Caligula of burglary in second degree since Chaerea's dog used doghouse as summer residence); *Rex v. Seneca,* 100 Misc. 2d 634, 640 n. 2, 392 N.Y.S.2d 861, 867 n.2 (Sup. Ct. N.Y. County 1979) (exonerating Seneca of third degree buglary where Nero's dog was too afraid to stay in doghouse at night).

The Government relies by analogy on the case *Rex v. Sphinx,* 65 N.Y.2d 805, 503 N.E.2d 601, 507 N.Y.S.2d 919 (1987). In *Sphinx,* Sphinx, a cat, was convicted of burglary in the third degree for reaching into Rameses' bird cage and stealing Rameses' swing. *Id.* at 807, 503 N.E.2d at 603, 507 N.Y.S.2d at 922. *Sphinx* is distinguishable from the case before this Court, however, because, unlike Roman Nose, Rameses lived in the cage at night although he did not do so during the day. *See id.*

Molotov Cocktail As "Incendiary Device"

We also find that a "Molotov cocktail" is an "incendiary device" within the meaning of section 150.20 of the Penal Law. *See* N.Y. Penal

Law § 150.20(2) (McKinney 1988). #16 Subdivision two of section 150.20 states that "as used in this section, 'incendiary device' means a breakable container designed to explode or produce uncontained combustion upon impact, containing flammable liquid and having a wick or a similar device capable of being ignited." *Id.*

Section 150.20 was amended in 1984 to add the definition of "incendiary device." Ch. 950, 2 [1984] N.Y. Laws 1426. The state legislature was concerned that individuals who hurled "Molotov cocktails" could not be found guilty of arson in the first degree which carries a stiffer penalty. #17 *See, e.g. Rex v. McCrawford*, 47 A.D.2d 318, 321, 366 N.Y.S.2d 424, 429 (1st Dep't 1975) (defendant, hurling "Molotov cocktail" through apartment window where alleged assailant of defendant lived, could not be convicted of arson under section 150.20 since "Molotov cocktail," although "incendiary device," not "explosive" as required by that section). Memorandum of Sen. Santucci, *reprinted in* [1984] N.Y. Legis. Ann. 145. In approving this amendment to the bill, the governor stated that "the unlawful use of 'incendiary devices,' as well as of 'explosives' in an occupied building, is a Nerodian deed evincing an extraordinary indifference to human life and deserving the maximum punishment of life imprisonment as provided for by this bill." Governor's Memorandum on Approval of ch. 950, N.Y. Laws (July 21, 1984), *reprinted in* [1984] N.Y. Legis. Ann. 145.

Conclusion

A final issue can be dealt with summarily. That Roman Nose's incessant practical joking led Julius Caesar to retaliate is not a defense to the crime of arson.[3] #18 *See e.g. Rex v. Caesar*, 58 A.D.2d 99, 101, 432 N.Y.S.2d 66, 68 (1st Dep't 1977) (Brutus rolling pair of dice each morning when Brutus and Julius Caesar would eat breakfast is not defense to Julius Caesar's setting fire to Brutus' home); *Rex v. Nero*, 77 A.D.2d 601, 606, 352 N.Y.S.2d 934, 936 (2d Dep't 1980) (Agrippina pulling Nero's hair to awaken Nero every time he was sleeping is not defense to Nero's ordering death of Agrippina or torching of her house).

The judgments of conviction are reversed. This Court would strongly urge Roman Nose to pursue all civil remedies available to him lest he be heard to utter those immortal words, "It's a dog's life."

---

[3]   Caesar admitted at trial that he was embittered by the incessant practical joking of Roman Nose and Cleopatra and by his inability to stop the joking through civil litigation.

Answers (Citation Exercise #9)

#1. Corrected Citation:

_____

_____

Rule(s): _____

_____

_____

#2. Corrected Citation:

_____

_____

Rule(s): _____

_____

_____

#3. Corrected Citation:

_____

_____

Rule(s): _____

_____

_____

#4. Corrected Citation:

_____

_____

Rule(s): _____

_____

_____

#5. Corrected Citation:

_____

_____

Rule(s): _____

_____

_____

#6. Corrected Citation:

_____

_____

Rule(s): _____

_____

_____

#7. Corrected Citation:

_____

_____

Rule(s): _____

_____

_____

#8. Corrected Citation:

_____

_____

Rule(s): _____

_____

_____

#9. Corrected Citation:

_____

_____

Rule(s): _____

_____

_____

#10.Corrected Citation:

_____

_____

    Rule(s): _____

_____

_____

#11. Corrected Citation:

_____

_____

    Rule(s): _____

_____

_____

#12.Corrected Citation:

_____

_____

    Rule(s): _____

_____

_____

#13.Corrected Citation:

_____

_____

    Rule(s): _____

_____

_____

#14.Corrected Citation:

_____

_____

    Rule(s): _____

_____

_____

#15. Corrected Citation:

_____

_____

Rule(s): _____

_____

_____

#16. Corrected Citation:

_____

_____

Rule(s): _____

_____

_____

#17. Corrected Citation:

_____

_____

Rule(s): _____

_____

_____

#18. Corrected Citation:

_____

_____

Rule(s): _____

_____

_____

Afterword

By now, you are well on your way to beating the citation blues. You have learned to crack the mysteries of the Bluebook and have acquired the skills needed to accurately produce and to properly place the basic citation forms you will use most often: cases, statutes, treatises, federal regulations and law review articles.

If you find yourself forgetting what you have learned, do not despair. You can refresh your skills by reviewing the exercises in this book. If you are having trouble with a particular citation form or if you have to write one for an authority you have never encountered before—it is impossible to introduce you to all the myriad of possible authorities in this small workbook—you can always turn to the index at the back of the Bluebook. The index is an alphabetical key to every citation form in the Bluebook, from federal cases to foreign constitutions to international treaties; it will guide you to that page of the Bluebook containing the rules for the citation form you are seeking.

We hope that this book will assure that the Bluebook never makes you blue again.

Thanks.

Appendix

Sample Trial Memorandum

This appendix contains a trial memorandum of law, sometimes referred to in popular parlance as a brief. The trial memorandum of law is very similar to the appellate brief, and can address a wide range of issues. The trial memorandum included here is written in opposition to a motion to dismiss and for summary judgment at the federal level.

Note that this trial memorandum of law does not include a statement of facts or the equivalent, but does include a preliminary statement. While not technically required in all cases, a preliminary statement is useful because it summarizes in one or two pages the essence of a party's argument(s). For this reason, it is very useful to a judge and the judge's clerk. Usually the preliminary statement is followed by a statement of facts; sometimes, however, when a court imposes strict and rigorous page limitations, the statement is foregone (except in summary form) and affidavits are solely relied upon to supply the factual information.

This trial memorandum of law was submitted to a judge in the federal district court for the Southern District of New York. Individual judges frequently have their own rules regarding page limitations and other matters pertinent to the submission of materials, the court calendar and the like. This judge imposed a twenty-five page limit on trial memoranda of law; the attorney requested a five-page extension which was—reluctantly—granted.

The trial memorandum of law is valuable to you because it is correctly "bluebooked." Please note two things about the memorandum: we included parallel citations for state cases and we cited to an encyclopedia, *New York Jurisprudence Second*, even though in practice you should only cite to an encyclopedia where it, like *New York Jurisprudence*, is a good one, and where, as here, it states a very important principle not stated elsewhere.

United States District Court
Southern District of New York

- X

S.S. BANK,   :

      Plaintiff and   :
      Counterclaim   :
      Defendant,   :

- against -   :   91 Civ. 5328 (JES)

RICHARD CIAMPI, RIVER   :
CORPORATION, and ATLANTIC   :
CORPORATION,   :

      Defendants and   :
      Counterclaimants.   :

- X

Memorandum of Law of Defendants and Counterclaimants in Opposition to the Motion for Summary Judgment and for Dismissal

Preliminary Statement

This Memorandum is submitted by defendants and counterclaimants Richard Ciampi ("Ciampi"), River Corporation ("River"), and Atlantic Corporation ("Atlantic") in opposition to the motion of plaintiff and counterclaim defendant S.S. Bank (the "Bank") for summary judgment pursuant to rule 56(c) of the Federal Rules of Civil Procedure ("Rule 56") and to dismiss for failure to state a claim pursuant to rule 12(b)(6) ("Rule 12(b)(6)"). The motion is based on alleged guaranties signed by Ciampi, River and Atlantic (individually, a "Guaranty," and collectively, the "Guaranties"), of a loan (the "Loan") of $4.9 million from the Bank to United States Vessels, Inc. ("U.S. Vessels") on or about November 15, 1989.

The Bank would have the Court believe that this case involves a simple action upon guaranties of a loan now in default. However, this is actually a serious case of fraud perpetrated upon Ciampi, River and Atlantic by the Bank in order to induce them to sign the Guaranties for the Loan from the Bank to U.S. Vessels, as the accompanying affidavits of Ciampi ("Ciampi Affidavit") and Jeffrey Begley ("Begley Affidavit") clearly demonstrate.

Point I

SUMMARY JUDGMENT IS PRECLUDED ON
THE PLAINTIFF'S CLAIMS AND ON THE
DEFENDANTS' DEFENSES AND COUNTERCLAIMS

Summary judgment will be granted only if the movant shows that there is no genuine issue as to any material fact, and that the movant is entitled to judgment as a matter of law. Fed. R. Civ. P. Rule 56(c); *Celotex Corp. v. Catrett*, 477 U.S. 317, 330 (1986) (Brennan, J., dissenting); *Anderson v. Liberty Lobby, Inc.*, 477 U.S. 242, 256 (1986). Summary judgment is a drastic procedural weapon because "'its prophylactic function, when exercised, cuts off a party's right to present his case to a jury.'" *Garza v. Marine Transp. Lines, Inc.*, 861 F.2d 23, 26 (2d Cir. 1988) (quoting *Donnelly v. Guion*, 467 F.2d 290, 291 (2d Cir. 1972)). The burden is on the moving party to show the absence of any genuine issue as to all of the material facts. *See Oxley v. City of New York*, 923 F.2d 22, 24 (2d Cir. 1991).

In deciding a motion for summary judgment, the "fundamental maxim" is that the Court "'cannot try issues of fact; it can only determine whether there are issues to be tried.'" *Donahue v. Windsor Locks Bd. of Fire Comm'rs*, 834 F.2d 54, 58 (2d Cir. 1987) (quoting *Heyman v. Commerce & Indus. Ins. Co.*, 524 F.2d 1317, 1319-20 (2d Cir. 1975)). Because summary judgment is such a drastic measure, the inferences to be drawn from the underlying facts contained in materials submitted on the motion for summary judgment must be viewed in the light against the movant and most favorable to the party opposing the motion. *Bishop v. Wood*, 426 U.S. 341, 347 n.11 (1976); *United States v. Diebold, Inc.*, 369 U.S. 654, 655 (1962). Furthermore, in determining whether a genuine issue has been raised, a court must resolve all ambiguities and draw all reasonable inferences against the moving party, and all doubts as to the existence of a genuine issue for trial should be resolved against the moving party. *Celotex*, 477 U.S. at 330 n.2; *Adickes v. Liberty Lobby, Inc.*, 398 U.S. 144, 158-59 (1970); *Donahue*, 834 F.2d at 57.

A. The Plaintiff Is Not Entitled To Judgment As A Matter Of Law That The Defendants Are Precluded From Raising Any Counterclaims Or Defenses In Respect Of The Guaranties.

The Bank is not entitled to summary judgment on its claims or on the defendants' defenses or counterclaims based on the defendants' alleged disclaimers because such disclaimers are too general and were not negotiated.

1. The Disclaimers In The Guaranties Are Too General.

The law is well-settled that fraud vitiates a contract since a "creditor cannot recover from a guarantor where the creditor has practiced any

fraud to induce the guarantor to assume to the obligation of the guaranty."
63 N.Y. Jur. 2d *Guaranty and Suretyship* § 171 (1987); *see also General
Motors Acceptance Corp. v. Kalstein*, 101 A.D.2d 102, 104, 474 N.Y.S.2d
493, 495 (1st Dep't 1984). It is also well-settled that "[p]arol evidence of
a fraudulent misrepresentation including a misrepresentation as to intent
is admissible to avoid an agreement induced by such fraud." *Millerton
Agway Coop. Inc. v. Briarcliff Farms, Inc.*, 17 N.Y.2d 57, 61, 215 N.E.2d
341, 343, 268 N.Y.S.2d 18, 21 (1966) (citing *Sabo v. Delman*, 3 N.Y.2d 155,
160-61, 153 N.E.2d 906, 909, 164 N.Y.S.2d 714, 716-17 (1957)); *see also
Abrams v. Xenon Indus., Inc.*, 145 A.D.2d 362, 535 N.Y.S.2d 616 (1st
Dep't 1988).

Even for an agreement with a general "merger" clause, New York
courts have held that the parol evidence rule does not bar proof of fraudulent misrepresentations. *See Crowell-Collier Publishing Co. v. Jose-
fowitz*, 5 N.Y.2d 998, 999, 157 N.E.2d 730, 731, 184 N.Y.S.2d 859, 860
(1959); *Sabo*, 3 N.Y.2d at 161, 153 N.E.2d at 910, 164 N.Y.S.2d at 717-18.
In this case, the Guaranties do not even contain a merger clause[1] or any
other language to bar parol evidence of fraudulent misrepresentations.

While the Guaranties are "absolute and unconditional," such language is not sufficient, by itself, to preclude proof of fraud in the inducement. *See Millerton Agway*, 17 N.Y.2d at 61, 215 N.E.2d at 343, 268
N.Y.S.2d at 21; *GTE Automatic Elec. Inc. v. Martin's Inc.*, 127 A.D.2d 545,
512 N.Y.S.2d 107, 108 (1st Dep't 1987). Furthermore, the additional disclaimer language in the Guaranties relied on by the Bank is not specific
enough to disclaim the contentions raised by defendants.[2]

In *Schneider v. OG & C Corp.*, 684 F. Supp. 1269 (S.D.N.Y. 1988), a
case involving language similar to that in the Guaranties, the district
court denied summary judgment on the ground that the language was not
sufficiently specific to disclaim certain defenses raised by the defendants.
Id. at 1273. Defendant OG & C Corporation ("OGC") defaulted on a loan

---

[1]   The absence of a merger clause in the Guaranties is consistent with the defendants' position that the Bank recognized the prior oral agreements between them. The
Bank refused to incorporate in any external document its promise to roll the Note over and
rely on the Collateral for repayment because it was concerned about its own possible tax
liability (*see* Begley Aff. at 8). The Bank, however, did not include in the Loan Documents
the standard "merger" clause, which would typically provide that (a) the Loan Agreement
superseded all prior agreements, including oral agreements, and (b) no representation or
promise had been made by the Bank other than in the Loan Documents.

[2]   *See Northwestern Nat'l Ins. Co. v. Alberts*, 717 F. Supp. 148 (S.D.N.Y. 1989);
Schneider v. OG & C Corp., 684 F. Supp. 1269 (S.D.N.Y. 1988); *BT Commercial Corp. v.
Blum*, 175 A.D.2d 43, 572 N.Y.S.2d 10 (1st Dep't 1991); *GTE Automatic Elec. Inc. v. Mar-
tin's Inc.*, 127 A.D.2d 545, 512 N.Y.S.2d 107 (1st Dep't 1987); *Goodridge v. Fernandez*, 121
A.D.2d 942, 505 N.Y.S.2d 144 (1st Dep't 1986).

made by plaintiffs and co-guaranteed by defendants Mersky and Tuchinsky. *Id.* at 1270. The guaranties stated:

> This Guaranty shall be construed as a continuing, absolute and unconditional guaranty of payment without regard to the validity, regularity or enforceability of any of the Obligations [of the principal debtor], . . . and without regard to any defense, set off or counterclaim which may at any time be available to or be asserted by the Debtor against Lender and which constitutes, or might be construed to constitute, an equitable or legal discharge of the Debtor for any of the Obligations, or the undersigned [guarantor] under this Guaranty, in bankruptcy or in any other instance. . . .

Id. at 1273. Plaintiffs sued on the note and the guaranties.

In opposition to summary judgment, Mersky and Tuchinsky interposed the defense of fraud, among other defenses. *Id.* They specifically challenged the validity of the guaranties on the ground of fraudulent misrepresentations to OGC and the guarantors during the negotiations among the parties. *Id.* at 1271-72.

The court found that the language of the guaranties was not specific enough to preclude a fraudulent inducement defense.[3] The court reasoned that Mersky and Tuchinsky did not specifically disclaim "*defenses based on their guaranties*," and, therefore, were not precluded from bringing the defense of fraud in the inducement in the signing of the guaranties. *Id.* at 1273 (emphasis added); *accord Goodridge v. Fernandez*, 121 A.D.2d 942, 945-46, 505 N.Y.S.2d 144, 147-48 (1st Dep't 1986) ("the guarantee here, . . . contains no specific disclaimer of defenses available to the guarantor

---

[3] The language was substantially the same as that in *Goodridge v. Fernandez*, 121 A.D.2d 942, 945-46, 505 N.Y.S.2d 144, 147-48 (1st Dep't 1986), a New York appellate case also denying summary judgment against a guarantor on an alleged "absolute and unconditional" guarantee. *See* 684 F. Supp. at 1272- 73. The language of the *Fernandez* guarantee is as follows:

> This Guarantee shall be construed as a continuing, absolute and unconditional guarantee of payment without regard to (i) the validity, regularity or enforceability of the [principal obligations], . . . (iv) any defense, setoff or counterclaim which may at any time be available to or asserted by [the debtor] against [the creditors], or (v) any other circumstance whatsoever (with or without notice to or knowledge of [the debtor] or the Guarantor) which constitutes, or might be construed to constitute, in bankruptcy or in any other instance, an equitable or legal discharge of [the debtor] for the Obligations or of the Guarantor under this Guarantee.

Id. at 1273 (quoting *Fernandez,* 121 A.D.2d at 946, 505 N.Y.S.2d at 147-48).

with respect to the guarantee") (emphasis added). Defendants' fraudulent inducement defenses in this case are with respect to the Guaranties.

Similarly, in *BT Commercial Corp. v. Blum*, 175 A.D.2d 43, 572 N.Y.S.2d 10 (1st Dep't 1991), the Appellate Division held that a disclaimer of "counterclaims" in a guaranty was not sufficiently specific to disclaim *defenses*. In *BT Commercial*, Federal Resources Corporation acquired Kenyon Home Furnishings. *Id.* The defendants executed guaranties with respect to a contract between the plaintiff and Kenyon Home Furnishings to make funds available to finance Kenyon's operation and expansion. *Id.* The guaranties provided that

> 2. Defendant(s) "unconditionally" and "irrevocably" guarantee payment of Kenyon's debts to BT Commercial Corporation to the extent set forth in each guaranty.
>
> 3. "No invalidity, irregularity or unenforceability of all or any part of the liabilities hereby guaranteed or of any security therefor shall affect, impair or be a defense to this guaranty. . . ."
>
> 4. "The undersigned . . . in the event of any litigation between the parties hereto in respect of any matter arising under this guaranty . . . agrees that . . . the undersigned will not interpose any counterclaims or setoff of any nature."

Id.

When Kenyon was in liquidation, plaintiff commenced an action against defendants on the guaranties. *Id.* Defendants asserted affirmative defenses, the two in issue before the court being those for negligence. *Id.* The trial court denied the plaintiff's motion pursuant to CPLR 3211 to dismiss defendants' affirmative defenses of negligence. *Id.* The Appellate Division affirmed, holding that

> [P]laintiff relies upon the decision by the Court of Appeals in *Citibank, N.A. v. Plapinger*, 66 N.Y.2d 90, for the proposition that defendants are precluded from asserting negligence as an affirmative defense to unconditional and irrevocable guaranties. Yet, it is significant that plaintiff's motion is for dismissal under CPLR 3211 and not one for summary judgment pursuant to section 3212. Since the two guaranties expressly prohibit defendants from advancing any counterclaim or setoff, but omit mention of a defense, it is unclear whether the instruments were also intended to bar them from interposing any defense as well. It is established that an ambiguity in a contract must be construed against the party who drafted it. . . .

Id.[4]

---

[4] Under *BT Commercial*, at the very least, the defendants' counterclaims in this case cannot be dismissed based on the disclaimer of *defenses* found in the Guaranties. Therefore, the Bank's motion with respect to the counterclaims should be denied.

Based on *Schneider* and *BT Commercial* the disclaimers in the Guaranties in this case do not, as a matter of law, preclude defendants' defenses with respect to the Guaranties or any of their counterclaims. The Guaranties in relevant parts merely state:

> The liability of the Guarantor under this Guaranty shall be absolute and unconditional irrespective of:

> (i) any lack of validity or enforceability of the Loan Agreement, the Note or any other Agreement or instrument relating thereto;
> . . .

> (vii) any other circumstance which might otherwise constitute a defense available to, or a discharge of, the Borrower or Guarantor.

Under *Schneider* and *Fernandez*, the disclaimer in the Guaranties is not sufficiently specific because it does not state that Ciampi, River and Atlantic disclaimed defenses and counterclaims *with respect to the Guaranties*. Likewise, under *BT Commercial*, the disclaimer in the Guaranties is at best ambiguous. Disclaimers of "counterclaims" (the language in *BT Commercial*) cannot disclaim defenses. Disclaimers of "defenses" (the language in the Guaranties) cannot disclaim counterclaims. Ambiguity must be construed against the Bank. Therefore, in any event, defendants' counterclaims would clearly withstand the motion for summary judgment under *BT Commercial*.[5]

---

[5] The court in *BT Commercial* stated that plaintiff's failure to bring a summary judgment motion is significant, suggesting that it could not do so precisely because the disclaimer is ambiguous enough to preclude summary judgment. *See* 175 A.D.2d at 43, 572 N.Y.S.2d at 10. Once ambiguity is introduced, either under the *Schneider* distinction or the *BT Commercial* distinction, parol evidence is admissible as to the defenses and counterclaims. The *Schneider* case specifically states this. *See Schneider*, 684 F. Supp. at 1274. Furthermore, the rules concerning ambiguous contract terms make this clear. "The parties have a right to present oral testimony or other extrinsic evidence at trial to aid in interpreting a contract whose provisions are not wholly unambiguous." *Heyman v. Commerce & Indus. Ins. Co.*, 524 F.2d 1317, 1320 (2d Cir. 1975); *see Foster Medical Corp. Employees' Pension Plan v. Healthco, Inc.*, 753 F.2d 194, 198 (1st Cir. 1985) (applying New York law). Parol evidence is admissible because it does not vary or contradict the written terms of the contract, but merely aids in their interpretation; the "parol is used to determine what the terms of the agreement are." *Garza v. Marine Transp. Lines, Inc.*, 861 F.2d 23, 27 (2d Cir. 1988); *Heyman*, 524 F.2d at 1320 n.2 (citing 3 Arthur Linton Corbin, *Contracts* § 579 (1960)). Contractual language is ambiguous if it "is susceptible of at least two fairly reasonable interpretations"; in such a case, "this presents a triable issue of fact, and summary judgment would be improper." *Aetna Casualty & Sur. Co. v. Giesow*, 412 F.2d 468, 471 (2d Cir. 1969); *United Brands Co. v. Intermediate Credit Corp.*, 426 F. Supp. 856, 861 (S.D.N.Y. 1977) (quoting *Aetna*) (summary judgment denied on claim on guarantee); *accord Garza*, 861 F.2d at 27; *Painton & Co. v. Bourns, Inc.*, 442 F.2d 216, 233 (2d Cir. 1971); *Lemelson v. Ideal Toy Corp.*, 408 F.2d 860, 863 (2d Cir. 1969).

Here, the disclaimers in the Guaranties clearly do not cover defenses with respect to the *Guaranties,* or any counterclaims. The *Bank* has raised the issue of ambiguity in trying to stretch the disclaimers to cover all counterclaims and defenses with respect to the Guaranties and, therefore, cannot prevail on a motion for summary judgment.

The *Schneider, Fernandez* and *BT Commercial* courts distinguished *Plapinger*,[6] which is relied on heavily by the Bank. In *Plapinger*, the defendants alleged, *inter alia*, fraud in the inducement, against five banks suing them on a guaranty. The banks' motion for summary judgment was granted by Special Term, which held that "by the specific language of the unconditional guarantee defendants waived their right to assert the defenses and counterclaims." 66 N.Y.2d at 92, 485 N.E.2d at 974, 495 N.Y.S.2d at 310. The Court of Appeals carefully reviewed the language of the particular guaranty in light of its prior holdings that a "general merger clause is ineffective to exclude parol evidence of fraud in the inducement," and held that an exception to this rule exists "where the person claiming to have been defrauded has by his own specific disclaimer of reliance upon oral representations himself been 'guilty of deliberately misrepresenting [his] true intention.'" *Id.* at 94, 485 N.E.2d at 975, 495 N.Y.S.2d at 311 (citation omitted).

The exact language used in the *Plapinger* guaranty is crucial to an analysis of that Court's holding and distinguishes it from the case at bar. That guaranty specifically stated that it was "absolute and unconditional irrespective of . . . any other circumstance which might otherwise constitute a defense available to, or a legal or equitable discharge of, the Borrower in respect of the Obligations or a surety or *guarantor in respect of this Shareholders' Guaranty* (it being agreed that the obligations of the Shareholder Guarantors hereunder shall not be discharged except by payment as herein provided)." Shareholders' Guaranty in *Plapinger*, annexed to the Bank's motion as Ex. C; *see* 66 N.Y.2d at 95, 485 N.E.2d at 976, 495 N.Y.S.2d at 312.

In its memorandum, the Bank attempts to mislead this Court by misquoting the very language of the *Plapinger* guaranty on which the decision in *Plapinger* rests. The Bank thereby distorts the meaning of the *Plapinger* guaranty by deleting language which distinguishes it from the Guaranties here. The Bank's memorandum states:

> Finally, the provisions of the *Plapinger* guaranty and Guaranties executed by the defendants here are virtually identical. Section 2 of the *Plapinger* guaranty provides:
>
>> Each Shareholder Guarantor guarantees that the Obligations will be paid strictly in accordance with the terms of the Amended and Restated Loan Agreement and the Notes, regardless of any law, regulation or order now or hereafter in effect in any jurisdiction affecting any of such terms or

---

[6]   In *Schneider,* Judge Conboy noted that the *Fernandez* decision "has added weight in that Justice Carro, who sat on the panel, . . . had participated in *Citibank, N.A. v. Plapinger* when that case was before the Appellate Division, First Department." 684 F. Supp. at 1273 n.10.

the rights of the Agent or the Banks with respect hereto. The liability of each Shareholder Guarantor under this Shareholders' Guaranty shall be absolute and unconditional irrespective of:

> (i) any lack of validity or enforceability of the Restated Guaranty, the Amended and Restated Loan Agreement, the Notes . . . or any other agreement or instrument relating thereto; . . . or
>
> (vii) any other circumstances which might otherwise constitute a defense available to, or a legal or equitable discharge of, *the Borrower . . . or a guarantor.*

(Pl.'s Mem. at 14-15 (emphasis added).) The Bank has incorrectly and disingenuously ended this quote on the word "guarantor," where the original language in the *Plapinger* guaranty ended with the words "*in respect of this Shareholders' Guaranty. . . .*" (*See* Pl.'s Mem. Ex. C at 5.)

This misquote by the Bank is significant because the Guaranties in this case are distinguishable from the Shareholders' Guaranty in *Plapinger* because the Guaranties here do not specifically disclaim defenses "available to a guarantor *in respect of the guarantee.*" 66 N.Y.2d at 92, 485 N.E.2d at 974, 495 N.Y.S.2d at 309 (emphasis added). The *Plapinger* decision clearly turned on this critical language, which the Bank has seen fit to delete in its memorandum. *See id.* at 95, 485 N.E.2d at 977, 495 N.Y.S.2d at 309, 312. In short, the language of the disclaimers is not "sufficiently specific to foreclose as a matter of law the defenses and counterclaims." *Id.* at 93, 485 N.E.2d at 975, 495 N.Y.S.2d at 310. The plaintiff's motion for summary judgment must therefore be denied.[7]

2. The Terms Of The Guaranties Were Not Negotiated.

If the foregoing discussion as to the exact meaning and ambiguity of the disclaimers in the Guaranties appears a bit obscure, defendants respectfully agree: this point is precisely defendants' main argument. The Bank's efforts to apply *Plapinger* to the disclaimers in the Guaranties is wholly inappropriate because these disclaimers are not highly refined provisions that have the specific meaning that the Bank would like to read into them to preclude the defendants from raising the Bank's fraudulent misconduct. Rather, the disclaimers are standard, general boilerplate provisions, identical to the form disclaimers used by Shearman & Sterling for its bank clients. (*See* Ex. A.) They were never discussed or changed, or probably even read by defendants. To read them as disclaimers of the

---

[7] The plaintiff's motion for summary judgment on the defendants' affirmative defenses and counterclaims must be denied as to the claims for tortious interference and for breach of fiduciary duty for an additional reason. The facts giving rise to these claims are post-*Plapinger* facts, that is, the defendants do not rely on the oral misrepresentations leading up to execution of the Loan Agreement and Guaranties, but on events subsequent to their execution.

fraud engaged in by the Bank and "deliberate misrepresentations" by defendants of their "true intention" is absurd. The *Plapinger* Court placed significant emphasis on the guaranty's language being *heavily negotiated* and *not boilerplate*,[8] further distinguishing it from the Guaranties before this Court. 66 N.Y.2d at 95, 485 N.E.2d at 976, 495 N.Y.S.2d at 311. The Court stated:

> The *Danaan* rule has been criticized as encouraging the use of boilerplate and likely to result in more verbose merger clauses (Calamari and Perillo, Contracts § 9-21 [2d ed.]; Note, 47 Cornell LQ 655), a sounder distinction being between a negotiated clause and a standard form clause (Calamari and Perillo, *loc. cit., supra*) . . . . But here we do not have the generalized boilerplate exclusion referred to by the commentators.

Id. at 95, 485 N.E.2d at 976-77, 495 N.Y.S.2d at 311-12.[9]

More recently, in *Federal Ins. Co. v. Mallardi*, 696 F. Supp. 875 (S.D.N.Y. 1988), the Court emphasized the "soundness" of the negotiated versus non-negotiated clause distinction. In *Mallardi*, the defendants purchased units in a real estate tax shelter, by delivery of promissory notes obligating annual installment payments, and the plaintiff provided an investor bond promising payment if the defendants defaulted. *Id.* at 877. The defendant/purchasers signed an Indemnity and Security Agreement, whereby they "absolute[ly] and unconditional[ly]" agreed to pay to

---

[8]   The language of the disclaimers in the Guaranties is boilerplate:

Standardized forms of guaranty often provide that the guarantor's obligations shall be absolute and unconditional, irrespective of "any circumstance which might otherwise constitute a legal or equitable discharge or defense by a guarantor." It is suggested that such a term may be so broad as to be unenforceable, perhaps on the ground of unconscionability.

Peter A. Alces, *The Efficacy of Guaranty Contracts in Sophisticated Commercial Transactions*, 61 N.C. L. Rev. 655, 663 n.49 (1983).

[9]   As stated by Calamari and Perillo:

[I]n New York . . . [a] general merger clause is not deemed to bar parol evidence of misrepresentations, but a specific merger clause disclaiming specific representations is deemed to bar such evidence . . . . At the root [of this distinction] is a tension between the seemingly reasonable proposition that parties by agreement ought to be able to provide that a purchaser is relying solely upon his own inspection and the also reasonable proposition that a party ought not by use of magic words insulate himself from fraud. The distinction doubtless will cause draftsmen of standard forms to draft lengthier, more verbose merger clauses. A sounder distinction . . . would be between a negotiated clause and a standard form clause.

John D. Calamari & Joseph M. Perillo, *Hornbook on the Law of Contracts* § 921, at 371-72 & n.23 (3d ed. 1987) (citing *Plapinger*).

the plaintiff/bonding agent, upon demand, all amounts paid by plaintiff.[10] *Id.* at 883.

The plaintiff brought an action against the defendant purchasers following their default on the purchase agreement and moved for summary judgment based on the Indemnity and Security Agreement. *Id.* The defendants asserted that they were fraudulently induced to buy their interests in the real estate partnership and that they did not negotiate the Indemnity and Security Agreement. *Id.* In denying the plaintiff's motion for summary judgment, the court focused on the *Plapinger* distinction between negotiated agreements and standard form clauses. *See id.* at 884. Without deciding, the Court stated that a "sound basis exists for distinguishing" between contracts whose provisions are negotiated and those whose provisions are not. *Id.* The Court further stated that, based on the defendants' contentions that the terms of the Indemnity and Security Agreement were not negotiated, it would be "hard pressed to find that defendants were 'guilty of deliberately misrepresenting . . . [their] true intention'" under *Plapinger. Id.*

Similarly here, there was no negotiation of the disclaimers in the Guaranties, and, therefore, *Plapinger* is inapposite. The Bank has not introduced a single fact to support its position that negotiations of the relevant clauses were sufficient to support a conclusion that if the defendants are allowed to introduce their contentions at trial, they would be guilty of "deliberately misrepresenting [their] true intention." Indeed, no such facts can be adduced because defendants have shown that the disclaimers were not negotiated at all. Thus this case falls short of the *Plapinger* rule in two ways: the disclaimers do not specifically cover the defendants' contentions that the Bank seeks to bar, and the disclaimers were, in any event, not negotiated. *Plapinger* would require both findings, and therefore, summary judgment must be denied.[11]

---

[10] Section 2(b) of the Indemnity and Security Agreement provided:

The Obligations of the Indemnitor hereunder are absolute and unconditional and will be paid or performed strictly in accordance with the terms hereof irrespective of (i) any lack of validity or enforceability of, or any amendment or other modifications of, or waiver with respect to, the Bond, the Note, the Subscription Agreement, this Agreement, the Partnership Agreement or any other Limited Partner's Note or Subscription Agreement, or Indemnity and Security Agreement or any agreement between the Partnership and the Bank or any other instrument or agreement relating to any thereof; . . . (vi) any other circumstance which might otherwise constitute a defense available to, or discharge of, the Indemnitor in respect of the Note or the Obligations (as hereinafter defined).

696 F. Supp. at 883.

[11] Summary judgment should be denied also because discovery is still at an early stage. In a similar case, *Hunt v. Bankers Trust Co.*, 689 F. Supp. 666 (N.D. Tex. 1987), the court, applying Texas and New York law, denied summary judgment to banks where discovery was at an early stage. *Id.* at 670. In *Hunt*, the banks brought counterclaims on a loan agreement, notes and guarantees. *Id.* The plaintiffs asserted numerous defenses, including

B. Defendants Are Seeking Through Their Defenses Merely To Enforce The Full Terms Of The Loan Agreement.

The Bank argues that the parol evidence rule precludes the modification of a written agreement by a contemporaneous oral agreement that would "contradict" the written document. The oral agreement between the Bank and defendants, however, does not "contradict" the written document. The Note was indeed a one-year note, but the Bank also agreed orally to roll over the Note for an additional two years if payment had not been received on the Australian Collateral.

When examined in light of the circumstances of the execution, in particular the tax issues raised at that time, the oral agreement does not "contradict" the written document. The oral agreement merely provided additional terms, an additional obligation on the part of the Plaintiff to roll over the Note in certain circumstances and otherwise look first to the Australian Collateral. Further, as described in footnote 1, *supra,* the Guaranties did not contain any "merger" clause. The Bank's oral agreement to roll over the Note, therefore, became part of the terms of the underlying Loan.

The rule of integration does not, as a matter of law, bar a side oral agreement arising for different reasons, such as the tax issues discussed in the accompanying affidavits. Although it is true, as the Bank states, quoting from a decision of this Court, in the footnote at page 10 of its memorandum, that "a contract which appears complete on its face is integrated as a matter of law," this is an incomplete statement of the law. It is clear, and this Court has also held, that "under New York law, *in the absence of a merger clause,* 'the court must determine whether or not there is an integration "by reading the writing in the light of surrounding circumstances, and by determining whether or not the agreement was one

---

fraud in the inducement based on oral representations made prior to closing the transactions. *Id.* at 671. The banks asserted that these defenses were barred by specific provisions in the agreements. *Id.*

The court denied summary judgment, stating, as one basis for its decision, "that discovery is yet at an early stage in this case, and Plaintiffs may not be required to support their defenses with detailed summary judgment proof until after an adequate opportunity to discover such evidence." *Id.* at 670. The court reasoned that discovery could supply proof of defenses to defeat the banks' claims. *Id.* In regard to the particular claim of fraud in the inducement, the court stated that summary judgment should be denied because it could not preclude at this early stage "the possibility . . . that after further discovery Plaintiffs might be able to offer proof of fraud in the inducement that might not be barred by these provisions." *Id.* at 674-75.

Similarly here, further discovery may elicit from the Bank evidence of the oral agreements and misrepresentations made to the defendants, as well as evidence that the Guaranties were intended to be integrated with the oral aspects of the transaction. Thus, summary judgment must be denied at this stage of the litigation.

which the parties would ordinarily be expected to embody in the writing.""" *Adler & Shaykin v. Wachner*, 721 F. Supp. 472, 476 (S.D.N.Y. 1988) (emphasis added)(citations omitted).

Indeed, the Bank is aware of this glaring omission in the Loan Documents. To compensate, the Bank points to the clause in the Loan Agreement that its terms may not be waived or amended unless in writing, and attempts to bootstrap this provision into a "merger" clause, (*see* Pl.'s Mem. at 11), but this provision refers to waivers and amendments *subsequent* to the Loan Agreement and does not preclude *simultaneous* or prior oral agreements that constitute *part of* the Loan Agreement.

Defendants' right to demand the enforcement of the complete Loan Agreement as agreed to among the parties has nothing, therefore, to do with the *Plapinger* principle that precludes a defense of fraud if such defense has been explicitly disclaimed.

Point II

THE PLAINTIFF'S MOTION TO DISMISS THE DEFENDANTS' BREACH OF FIDUCIARY DUTY AND TORTIOUS INTERFERENCE CLAIMS MUST BE DENIED

The party moving to dismiss under Rule 12(b)(6) has the burden of demonstrating that no claim has been stated. *See Johnsrud v. Carter*, 620 F.2d 29, 33 (3d Cir. 1980). The Court must presume all factual allegations of the complaint to be true and make all reasonable inferences in favor of the non-moving party. *Miree v. DeKalb County*, 433 U.S. 25, 27 n.2 (1977); *Scheuer v. Rhodes*, 416 U.S. 232, 236 (1974); *Murray v. City of Milford*, 380 F.2d 468, 470 (2d Cir. 1967). Furthermore, the allegations of the complaint (or, in this case, the counterclaims) are to be liberally construed. *See Schlesinger Inv. Partnership v. Fluor Corp.*, 671 F.2d 739, 742-43 (2d Cir. 1982).

A pleading should not be dismissed for failure to state a claim unless it appears "beyond doubt that the plaintiff can prove no set of facts in support of his claim which would entitle him to relief." *Conley v. Gibson*, 355 U.S. 41, 45-46 (1957); *Build of Buffalo, Inc. v. Sedita*, 441 F.2d 284, 287 (2d Cir. 1971); *see also Lynn v. Valentine*, 19 F.R.D. 250, 252 (S.D.N.Y. 1956) (same rule applies to counterclaims). Moreover, the likelihood that a party will prevail is irrelevant; as the Supreme Court stated in *Scheuer*:

> When a federal court reviews the sufficiency of a complaint, before the reception of any evidence either by affidavit or admissions, its task is necessarily a limited one. The issue is not whether a plaintiff will ultimately prevail but whether the claimant is entitled to offer evidence to support the claims.

Indeed it may appear on the face of the pleadings that a recovery is very remote and unlikely but that is not the test.

416 U.S. at 236; *accord Goldman v. Belden,* 754 F.2d 1059, 1067 (2d Cir. 1985).

The Bank cannot demonstrate that the defendants cannot prove any set of facts in support of their counterclaims for breach of fiduciary duty or for tortious interference. Thus, the Bank's motion to dismiss these claims must be denied.

A. Defendants Have Stated A Claim For Breach Of Fiduciary Duty.

While the relationship between a lender and a borrower or guarantor is ordinarily that of creditor and debtor and is not a fiduciary relationship, in some cases this relationship does result in fiduciary duties on the part of the lender. *See Reid v. Key Bank,* 821 F.2d 9, 17 (1st Cir. 1987); *Weinberger v. Kendrick,* 698 F.2d 61, 79 (2d Cir. 1982), *cert. denied sub nom. Lewy v. Weinberger,* 464 U.S. 818 (1983); *High v. McLean Fin. Corp.,* 659 F. Supp. 1561, 1568 (D.D.C. 1986); *In re Teltronics Servs.,* 29 B.R. 139, 171 (Bankr. E.D.N.Y. 1983); *Steelvest Inc. v. Scansteel Serv. Center Inc.,* 807 S.W.2d 476, 485 (Ky. 1991); *M.L. Stewart & Co. v. Marcus,* 124 Misc. 86, 207 N.Y.S. 685 (Sup. Ct. N.Y. County 1924). One such circumstance is a party's reposing confidence and trust in a bank.[12]

Fiduciary principles were long ago applied to lenders if an actual relationship of trust and confidence existed. *See Stewart v. Phoenix Nat'l Bank,* 49 Ariz. 34, ___, 64 P.2d 101, 103 (1937); *Barrett v. Bank of America,* 183 Cal. App. 3d 1362, 1364, 229 Cal. Rptr. 16, 18 (Ct. App. 1986); *Steelvest,* 807 S.W.2d at 484.

Under New York law, the relationship between pledgor and pledgee is one of trust, particularly with regard to the pledged collateral. *Kono v. Roeth,* 237 A.D. 252, 253, 260 N.Y.S. 662, 664-65 (1st Dep't 1932); *see Toplitz v. Bauer,* 161 N.Y. 325, 327, 55 N.E. 1059, 1061 (1900); *Gillet v. Bank of Am.,* 160 N.Y. 549, 560, 55 N.E. 292, 299 (1899). Under both com-

---

[12] It has also been held that a fiduciary relationship may arise in certain circumstances based on the lender's control over the other party. *See Hunt v. Bankers Trust Co.,* 689 F. Supp. 666, 675 (N.D. Tex. 1987) (applying New York and Texas law); *Beneficial Commercial Corp. v. Murray Glick Datsun, Inc.,* 601 F. Supp. 770, 772 (S.D.N.Y. 1985) (dismissing fiduciary duty claims as unsupported by facts); *In re Teltronics Servs.,* 29 Bankr. at 171. As argued herein, the fact that (1) the Bank knew the underlying $4.9 million loan could not be paid from borrower's operations in one year and would be looking for repayment to the Collateral, (2) exercised such complete control over the Collateral so as to be able to refuse to dispose of it and also refuse to allow the defendants to dispose of it, and (3) as a result, controlled the defendants' ability to engage in another financial transaction, the Hawaiian transaction for the Hawaii project, requires the Bank to be held to a higher, fiduciary standard.

mon law and the Uniform Commercial Code, the pledgee, or secured party, has a duty to "use reasonable care in the custody and preservation of collateral in his possession." N.Y. U.C.C. Law § 9-207(1) (McKinney 1991); *see Federal Deposit Ins. Corp. v. Frank L. Marino Corp.*, 74 A.D.2d 620, 622, 425 N.Y.S.2d 34, 36 (2d Dep't 1980); *Willets v. Hatch*, 132 N.Y. 41, 46, 30 N.E. 251, 256 (1892); *Grace v. Sterling, Grace & Co.*, 30 A.D.2d 61, 66, 289 N.Y.S.2d 632, 637 (1st Dep't 1968); Restatement (Security) § 17 (1941). The duty to exercise reasonable care in the preservation and protection of the collateral "exists as an incident to the possession and control of the goods or securities by the pledgee." *Grace*, 30 A.D.2d at 61, 289 N.Y.S.2d at 638. Further, a failure to preserve the pledge and refrain from impairing its value states a claim for breach of fiduciary duty. *Cf. Trans-Global Alloy, Ltd. v. First Nat'l Bank*, 583 So. 2d 443 (La. 1991) (where bank allowed letter of credit used as collateral to expire, jury could find that bank breached fiduciary duty to borrower); *Frank L. Marino Corp.*, 74 A.D.2d at 621, 425 N.Y.S.2d at 35-36 ("[w]here, . . ., a demand is made of the creditor to liquidate the collateral and subsequent to the refusal to liquidate the collateral substantially declines in value, the failure to liquidate, if negligent, is a breach of the secured party's duty to use reasonable care in the custody and preservation of collateral").

A bank's duty to preserve collateral continues after default on the principal obligation. U.C.C. § 9-207 cmt. 4 (1989). While not required to elect a remedy upon default,

> [t]his does not mean, however, that the bank owes no duties to defendant with respect to the collateral. It would be unfair to allow a creditor to deprive the debtor of the possession and use of the collateral for an unreasonable length of time and not apply the asset or the proceeds from its sale toward liquidation of the debt. Moreover, it would be equally unfair to allow a creditor to take possession at all, if the creditor never intended to dispose of the security. For during the period that the debtor is deprived of possession he may have been able to make profitable use of the asset or may have gone to far greater lengths than the creditor to sell. Once a creditor has possession he must act in a commercially reasonable manner toward sale, lease, proposed retention where permissible, or other disposition. If such disposition is not feasible, the asset must be returned, still subject, of course, to the creditor's security interest. To the extent the creditor's inaction results in injury to the debtor, the debtor has a right of recovery.

Michigan Nat'l Bank v. Marston, 29 Mich. App. 99, ___, 185 N.W.2d 47, 51 (1970) (citations omitted); *accord Henderson Few & Co. v. Rollins Communications, Inc.*, 148 Ga. App. 139, ___, 250 S.E.2d 830, 832 (1978);

Farmers State Bank v. Ballew, 626 P.2d 337, 340 (Okla. Ct. App. 1981); *Farmers State Bank v. Otten*, 87 S.D. 161, ____, 204 N.W.2d 178, 181 (1973).

Moreover, a bank's fiduciary duty prohibits impairing collateral if such impairment can damage a contract with a third party of which the bank is aware. For example, in *Trans-Global Alloy Ltd. v. First Nat'l Bank*, 583 So. 2d 443 (La. 1991), the Louisiana Supreme Court held a bank liable for breach of fiduciary duty because of its failure to preserve the value of a letter of credit held as loan collateral. *Id.* at 446.

In this case, the Bank, as pledgee and secured party under the pledge of the Collateral, owed a fiduciary duty to preserve and protect the Collateral. As part of this duty, after determining that U.S. Vessels allegedly defaulted, the Bank was prohibited from depriving the defendants of the possession and use of the Collateral for an unreasonable length of time while also refusing to foreclose. Moreover, the Bank's duty was enhanced because it knew that by tying up the Collateral, the commitment for the Hawaiian financing would expire. Clearly, the Bank has breached its fiduciary duty.

Although the Loan allegedly went into default on November 15, 1990, the Bank has not sought to repossess, dispose of, or allow the defendants the use of the Collateral. Indeed, when the Bank's repudiation of its covenant to roll the Note over and its unwillingness to negotiate any settlement became clear, the Bank still refused the defendants' request to liquidate the Collateral. As the Begley Affidavit demonstrates, in early 1991, U.S. Vessels and the defendants suggested that the Bank act to foreclose on the Collateral. On March 22, 1991, River delivered to the Bank's local Colorado counsel 25 documents, constituting substantially all of the documents necessary for such counsel to begin proceedings to foreclose on the Collateral and thus to repay the Loan. (Answer and Countercl. ¶ 33; Begley Aff. ¶ 28.) By letter dated April 4, 1991, the General Counsel of River acceded to the procedure proposed by the Bank for foreclosing on the Collateral. However, without having delivered any satisfactory written explanation, the Bank failed to proceed against it. Further, upon instituting this action, counsel to the Bank stated that during the pendency of this action, the Bank would not permit River to foreclose on the Collateral. (Answer and Countercl. ¶ 34; Begley Aff. ¶ 29-30.)

The Bank's failure to settle the Loan dispute, by rolling over the Note or foreclosing on the Collateral, has caused the Hawaiian takeout financing arrangement to fall through. The Bank was notified, and had full knowledge of, the negotiations between Atlantic and Hawaiian Bank, the letter of commitment from Hawaiian Bank, and subsequently the condition to the closing imposed by Hawaiian Bank that, on or prior to May 15, 1991, all alleged defaults relating to the Loan from the Bank would have to be cured and evidence of future performance of such obligations would have to be delivered. Notwithstanding this notice and knowledge, the Bank improperly and unjustifiably refused to foreclose, or allow defendants to foreclose, on the Colorado Property and thereby make full payment of all sums properly due and owing to the Bank. The result was the inability of Atlantic to close with Hawaiian Bank.[13] (Answer and Countercl. ¶ 32; Begley Aff. ¶ 24-26.)

It is clear from the discussion above that the defendants have stated a "set of facts in support of [their] claim which would entitle [the]m to relief." *Conley v. Gibson*, 355 U.S. 41, 45-46 (1957). The defendants allege that, based on the particular circumstances in this case, the Bank owed them a fiduciary duty to preserve and protect the Collateral and that it breached this duty by: (1) refusing to liquidate it; (2) holding it for an unreasonable length of time while not applying it or the proceeds from its sale toward liquidation of U.S. Vessels' debt; and (3) refusing to liquidate the collateral or to otherwise settle the Loan dispute with complete knowledge that the Hawaiian financing commitment for the Hawaiian project would fail. The motion to dismiss the claim for breach of fiduciary duty must therefore be denied.

B. The Defendants Have Stated A Claim For Tortious Interference.

The elements of the tort of interference with contractual or precontractual relations are: (i) the existence of a valid contract or a prospective contractual relationship; (ii) knowledge of the contract or prospective contractual relationship; (iii) intentional and unjustified interference with the contract or prospective contractual relationship; and (iv) damages. *See Israel v. Wood Dolson Co.*, 1 N.Y.2d 116, 120, 134 N.E.2d 97, 101, 151 N.Y.S.2d 1, 5 (1956); *S & S Hotel Ventures Ltd. Partnership v. 777 S.H. Corp.*, 108 A.D.2d 351, 353, 489 N.Y.S.2d 478, 480 (1st Dep't 1985); *Harden, S.P.A. v. Commodore Elecs., Ltd.*, 90 A.D.2d 733, 735, 455 N.Y.S.2d 792, 794 (1st Dep't 1982). Defendants have sufficiently alleged each element of their claim.

First, on May 15, 1990, the defendants received a letter of commitment from Hawaiian Bank to finance the Hawaiian project, which constituted a binding agreement even though conditions to funding were imposed. *See S & S Hotel Ventures*, 108 A.D.2d at 352-53, 489 N.Y.S.2d at 479-81. Even if the defendants were still negotiating with Hawaiian Bank, the contractual negotiations would be a sufficient basis for an

---

[13] Indeed, on or about April 22, 1991, the Bank was informed that the Hawaiian financing commitment had been extended only until May 15, 1991, in order to allow satisfaction of the final closing conditions, including the extension or settlement of the Loan. Fifteen days after the expiration of the extended commitment, the defendants learned that supervision of the Loan had been turned over to a new loan officer. The Hawaiian project continues to be without takeout financing.

action for tortious interference with prospective business relationships. *See CBS, Inc. v. Ahern*, 108 F.R.D. 14, 26-27 (S.D.N.Y. 1985).

Second, the Bank knew of the Hawaiian negotiations and the letter of commitment since as early as September 1990. The Bank also knew that Hawaiian required that the problem of the alleged Loan default be cured before Hawaiian would make its loan to the defendants.

Third, the Bank intentionally and unjustifiably interfered with the defendants' contract with Hawaiian Bank. Tortious interference is actionable in New York "if the [tortfeasor's] sole purpose is to damage the plaintiff or if the means employed to induce termination of the relationship are dishonest, unfair or otherwise improper." *Harden*, 90 A.D.2d at 735, 455 N.Y.S.2d at 794. Even if a party alleges justification for its interference, the use of wrongful means on its part may satisfy this element. *See S & S Hotel Ventures*, 108 A.D.2d at 354, 489 N.Y.S.2d at 481. Such wrongful means include breach of fiduciary duty or other violation of a relationship of confidence. *See A.S. Rampbell, Inc. v. Hyster Co.*, 3 N.Y.2d 369, 373, 144 N.E.2d 371, 376-77, 165 N.Y.S.2d 475, 481-82 (1957); *Mayo, Lynch & Assocs., Inc. v. Fine*, 148 A.D.2d 425, 426, 538 N.Y.S.2d 579, 580 (2d Dep't 1989). In addition, threats, intimidation or sharp practice may constitute the wrongful means. *See Lurie v. New Amsterdam Casualty Co.*, 270 N.Y. 379, 380, 1 N.E.2d 472, 473 (1936); *Katz v. Thompson*, 19 Misc. 2d 848, 852, 189 N.Y.S.2d 982, 985-86 (Sup. Ct. Westchester County), *aff'd*, 9 A.D.2d 951, 196 N.Y.S.2d 578 (2d Dep't 1959).

Further, a secured creditor's unreasonable withholding of consent which causes a debtor's business deal to collapse sufficiently states a claim for tortious interference under New York law. *See S & S Hotel Ventures*, 108 A.D.2d at 352, 489 N.Y.S.2d at 480. Defendants here have alleged the use of unjustifiable and improper means by the Bank, including breach of fiduciary duty and lack of cooperation and obstreperousness, and, additionally, that, as in *S & S Hotel Ventures*, the Bank unreasonably withheld its consent to resolve the Loan dispute by either rolling the Notes over or foreclosing on the Collateral, knowing that the deadline on the commitment letter from Hawaiian Bank would expire and the takeout financing would collapse. Furthermore, as alleged, the Bank took preliminary steps to foreclose on the Collateral and its subsequent refusal was an unjustified attempt to extract payments to which the Bank was not entitled. (Answer and Countercl. ¶ 34; Begley Aff. ¶ 29.) These improper means negate any "justification" the Bank may claim it has.

At this stage of the action, whether or not the standard of proof to be applied to defendants' claim that the Bank's actions *caused* the Hawaiian Bank financing to collapse is "strict," as the Bank alleges, is beside the point, and does not come close to establishing that this counterclaim should be dismissed prior even to the Bank's answering it. The Hawaiian deal was past the preliminary negotiation stage; an executed binding letter of commitment had been delivered to Atlantic. *See S & S Hotel Ventures*, 108 A.D.2d at 352, 489 N.Y.S.2d at 479. Other correspondence from Hawaiian Bank indicated explicitly that resolving the dispute with the Bank was a primary concern. Ultimately, Hawaiian Bank cited the failure to resolve the Loan dispute as a reason for the collapse of its financing commitment. In the absence of a responsive pleading from the Bank, it is clear that defendants have adequately and sufficiently pleaded a case for tortious interference.

The Bank relies disingenuously on a disembodied quote taken out of context from *Optivision Inc. v. Syracuse Shopping Ctr. Assoc.*, 472 F. Supp. 665, 685 (N.D.N.Y. 1979), for the proposition that its motion to dismiss defendants' counterclaim for tortious interference here should be granted if it is "'not absolutely clear that the negotiations would have been successfully concluded.'" The Bank neglects to mention that the issue in *Optivision* was whether the plaintiff had met its burden of showing "a probability of success" for the purpose of obtaining a *preliminary injunction*;[14] it has absolutely no application here, where, for purposes of its *motion to dismiss*, the Bank has not joined issue or even submitted affidavits or evidence upon which such determination could be made.

Finally, defendants have alleged damages resulting from the Bank's tort. Indeed, not only did the Hawaiian financing commitment fall through as a result of the Bank's actions, but the Hawaiian project also today continues to be without takeout financing, and Hawaiian is seeking to recover up to $1,000,000 in commitment fees and related costs.

---

[14] "[A]lthough the [*Optivision*] court found that the negotiations would not necessarily have resulted in a contract, it made those findings only after an evidentiary hearing on a motion for a preliminary injunction." *CBS, Inc. v. Ahern*, 108 F.R.D. at 27 n.23.

Conclusion

For each of the foregoing reasons, plaintiff's motion to dismiss and for summary judgment must be denied in all respects.

Dated: January 7, 1992

Respectfully submitted,

AKABAS & COHEN

By:_____
     Richard B. Cohen (5103)

Attorneys for Defendants
and Counterclaimants
1500 Broadway
New York, New York 10036
(212) 869-2249